The American Mind:

The Answer

by Buzz Shahan

THE AMERICAN MIND: THE ANSWER

Copyright © 2023 Buzz Shahan

First Edition: 2023

All rights reserved. No part of this publication may be reproduced, distributed, or transmitted in any form or by any means, including photocopying, recording, or other electronic or mechanical methods, without the prior written permission of the publisher, except in the case of brief quotations embodied in critical reviews and certain other noncommercial uses permitted by copyright law.

This book is a work of non-fiction. The author has made every effort to ensure that the accuracy of the information in this book was correct at the time of the publication. Neither the author nor the publisher nor any other person(s) associated with this book may be held liable for any damages that may result from any of the ideas made by the author in this book.

ISBN-13: 978-1-959677-23-9 (Paperback)
ISBN-13: 978-1-959677-22-2 (eBook)

Cover: Signing of the Declaration of Independence, giving birth to the American Mind, surrounded by the Star-Spangled Banner that hung over Fort McHenry on September 14, 1812.

Published by Defiance Press & Publishing, LLC

Bulk orders of this book may be obtained by contacting Defiance Press & Publishing, LLC. www.defiancepress.com.

Public Relations Dept. – Defiance Press & Publishing, LLC
281-581-9300
pr@defiancepress.com

Defiance Press & Publishing, LLC
281-581-9300
info@defiancepress.com

To my wife, Susan, and daughter, Mikki, whose editorial efforts are greatly appreciated.

About the Cover:

Signing of the Declaration of Independence, giving birth to the American Mind, surrounded by the Star-Spangled Banner that hung over Fort McHenry on September 14, 1812.

Table of Contents

Foreword 7
Introduction 11

SECTION 1: INTO THE AMERICAN MIND

Chapter 1: Components of the Mind.. 15
Chapter 2: A Work of Art 21
Chapter 3: Objectivity – The Pathway to Truth and Clear Thinking 27

SECTION 2: MORAL, RATIONAL, AND GOOD AND BAD

Chapter 4: Moral Agency 41
Chapter 5: Adam Smith and Rational Self-Interest 47

SECTION 3: BELIEF AND THE AMERICAN MIND

Chapter 6: Belief's Consequences.. 59
Chapter 7: Freedom, Independence, and Personal Progress......... 71

SECTION 4: RELIGION AND THE AMERICAN MIND

Chapter 8: Religion 101 81
Chapter 9: Ancient Architects – Abraham to Constantine 89
Chapter 10: Modern Architects – Luther to America 107
Chapter 11: Religion and Character 121
Chapter 12: Albert Einstein, Infinity, and God and Man 131

SECTION 5: Standards, Challenges, and Examples................... 139

Chapter 13: Standards and Character....................................... 141
Chapter 14: Sex and Character 149
Chapter 15: Drugs and the Mind 159
Chapter 16: Presidential Examples.. 169

Additional Points to Ponder... 177
About the Author 187
Additional Reading.. 191

Table of Contents

Foreword 7
Introduction 11

SECTION 1: INTO THE AMERICAN MIND

Chapter 1: Components of the Mind 15
Chapter 2: A Work of Art 21
Chapter 3: Objectivity – The Pathway to Truth and Clear Thinking 27

SECTION 2: MORAL, RATIONAL, AND GOOD AND BAD

Chapter 4: Moral Agency 41
Chapter 5: Adam Smith and Rational Self-Interest 47

SECTION 3: BELIEF AND THE AMERICAN MIND

Chapter 6: Belief's Consequences 59
Chapter 7: Freedom, Independence, and Personal Progress 71

SECTION 4: RELIGION AND THE AMERICAN MIND

Chapter 8: Religion 101 81
Chapter 9: Ancient Architects – Abraham to Constantine 89
Chapter 10: Modern Architects – Luther to America ... 107
Chapter 11: Religion and Character 121
Chapter 12: Albert Einstein, Infinity, and God and Man 131

SECTION 5: Standards, Challenges, and Examples 139

Chapter 13: Standards and Character 141
Chapter 14: Sex and Character 149
Chapter 15: Drugs and the Mind 159
Chapter 16: Presidential Examples 169

Additional Points to Ponder 177
About the Author 187
Optional Reading 191

Foreword

As the United States of America moves about the world stage, people outside her borders look at her and ask, *"Why is America different from where I live? How did that happen?"*

America is different from any civilization the world has ever known—and *remarkably* different. She is different because of the way she thinks, a way of thinking that had been crystalizing within English and European minds for some time prior to making its way across the Atlantic. She is different because her founders grasped the value of this way of thinking, this way of seeing the world, of seeing life itself, and embodied that concept in her founding.

Compared to what a global counterpart might expect from life, the difference between what an American expects from life can be so great that knowing what causes that difference is worthy of investigation. This is that investigation.

Recall that during England and Europe's New World colonization, France, Portugal, Spain, and England were all attempting to settle colonies in North and South America at the same time. In that colonization, each nation brought with it its philosophical view of life manifested principally in its governing principles. So, which culture ultimately won out? While Spain and Portugal hung on in the South and France in the North, England's influence in what was to become the United States of America overwhelmed the others.

It was not a purely English culture that took root in the future United States; it was a hybrid civilization largely based upon English law but heavily influenced by Protestant idealism. Incorporated within that idealism were certain behavioral mores expected from each citizen that shaped American society's evolving structure as well as the life outcome that a citizen could expect from that structure.

While harsh impositions like wearing a scarlet letter or enduring stocks in the public square physically imposed portions of this discipline upon adults, the fable of young George Washington confessing to chopping down his father's cherry tree took the same code all the way down to children.[1] Reviewing founder biographies, those that observed larger portions of those ideals prospered to greater degrees than those observing lesser portions, and prosperity includes not just material goods but slices of life's greatest joys.

While these ideals are no longer corporally imposed but self-imposed, assemble a set of parents that employ them, and you have a thriving family; enough businesses and you have a booming economy; enough individuals and you have a flourishing society; assemble them all and you have the United States of America.

So, what force lies at the foundation of these guiding principles? Emerging as a nation, United States' founders wove God himself into America's original political documents and governing philosophy. The view that God was not only the source of human life but Divine Grantor of the rights to which human life is entitled focused law and

---

1. *"Father, I cannot tell a lie: I cut down the tree!"* As the myth goes, when George Washington was six years old, he received a hatchet as a birthday gift and chopped down his father's newly planted cherry tree.

public policy upon His children as aspiring and independent individuals, not upon the state nor upon its administrators.

It became clear as this investigation progressed that, as a gardener tending plants must apply certain agronomic principles to maximize plant prosperity, America's original life-management principles facilitate human prosperity in the same way. It turns out that prospering Americans not only seek but demand the opportunity to live these principles. Why? Because, among all factors occurring within life's passage, improving one's life circumstances tops the list of individual aspirations. Search human history however you will, and you will find no behavioral code that comes close to advancing the individual's life compared to how original American cannon prescribes it.

This news falls hard on some ears: *"You're not going to tell me how to live my life, are you? You're not going to tell me that I must obey a certain moral code, are you?"* No, this book does not tell one how to manage one's life any more than a book on gardening insists that certain agronomic methods must be obeyed. Rather, if it were a book on gardening, it would list those conventions most likely to maximize a plant's prosperity. Whether or not to use such methods remains the choice of the gardener. The consequence of following a particular gardening method, however, ceases at some point to be a choice; harvest will be what it will be.

No matter what one's opinion of gardening might be, what gardener plants a seed without hope of it sprouting and maximizing its potential at harvest time? What person awakens to a new day without hope of advancement by day's end? Because America's founders understood the principles that had advanced their own and their family members' individual lives and fortunes, they structured a government not only inclusive of, but protective of, those same principles.[2] As a result, America soon soared above other world powers in every societal

---

2. Scripture: *"Man is that he might have joy."*

category and did so precisely because of those principles uncovered herein. Evidenced throughout America's fiercely spirited history, each principle upon which America was founded yields a rewarding promise. So, what are those principles and corresponding promises?

Introduction

Today, with one-fourth of China's population, America boasts a GDP nearly double that of second-ranked China. Her entrepreneurship in areas of medical, digital, and aero-space technology; education; the arts; agriculture; and science, has stood globally unmatched for the past century and a half. Her generosity in blood and treasure spent liberating the families of oppressed nations knows no equal. For opportunity to advance one's life, look no further. For sheer social vigor, look no further.

So, what caused the American phenomenon and continues causing it? At the heart of it all, America is America because the American citizen interprets and manages life's surroundings with an eye always toward making life better tomorrow than it was today, and this includes being an ever-nobler human being as well. That is why a person immigrates to the United States in the first place—to make a better life and to become a better person. Once here, a carrier of these desires meets, marries, and reproduces with someone doing the same thing. Their offspring, then, come loaded with ever-increasing quantities of the desire to make things better, and to be better, that such crystallizes into genetic occurrence.

So many now carry this gene that, despite the American Left's obliviousness to it, or misunderstanding of it, including outright hostility toward it, America will continue to soar. Also, because of this now biological entrenchment, the world will forever benefit from something that did not exist prior to America's founding and something that will never go away: It is the *American Mind*.[3]

This way of thinking is what Benjamin Franklin became and what guided America's founding. It is what brought Alexander Hamilton back from the brink but had little influence over the man who killed him. As the United States grew, these same thought processes guided the determined personalities of America's most notable presidents, namely George Washington, Andrew Jackson, Abraham Lincoln, Teddy Roosevelt, Harry Truman, and Ronald Reagan.

Understanding the origins of this historically novel way of dealing with one's surroundings makes clear how millions of Americans achieved, and continue to achieve, far greater meaning than their birth circumstance would have predicted. Striking is that through this method one need not be born into privilege to achieve privilege; one need not be handed a fortune to acquire one; one need not receive patronage to earn celebrity; and one need not be gifted to acquire great gifts. There is no magic nor mysticism to it. All one needs to soar through life is to achieve an *American Mind*. The whole proceeds from there.

---

3. Decades after drafting the Declaration of Independence, Thomas Jefferson declared its contents to be *"an expression of the American mind."*

Section 1
Into the American Mind

A journey into the American Mind begins with a review of those intangible elements that make up every human mind, which are: *Life energy, intellect, and emotion.*

We will see that the discipline of *objectivity* guides these unseen mental elements in their search for truth, and that truth is life's greatest discernment. Why is truth life's greatest discernment? Because discerning the truth of an issue leads to mastery of that issue.

Every human life faces issues—difficulties—that must be mastered before that life can advance to the next level. Such is life's process: an unending succession of challenging inclines and gentler plateaus.

The late comedic genius, Gilda Radner, facing the incline of ovarian cancer that would take her life, titled her autobiography written amidst her illness: *It's Always Something*.

Regardless of what that *something* happens to be in the moment, of where in life one is—young or aged; rich or poor; gifted or not so gifted; privileged or not so privileged; struggling or prospering; facing illness or basking in health—another incline is just around the corner. While one individual may be victimized by an incline, another will turn that same incline into victory. This begs the question: When facing the same challenge, what mental factors differentiate a conqueror's mind from that of a victim?

Not to be defeated but to defeat; not to be routed but to rout; not to be overcome but to overcome; not to slumber but to awaken; not to repose but to act. Drop any one of life's many obstacles into the path of an American Mind, and it will find its best solution. So, how did the American Mind get like that, and why are its social outcomes so different from those sponsored by societies with different beginnings?

Chapter 1
Components of the Mind

*W*hether one's mind follows Judeo-Christianity as its standard for behavioral comparison, or Islam, or Buddhism, or Hinduism, or a godless political creed like Communism; whether one's mind accepts fidelity as part of the marriage standard and whether one's mind can balance a budget, all these determinations take place within complicated thought processes.

Whether in executing these thought processes, a mind sees itself as divinely eternal or believes that it only exists between birth and death, the human mind is made up of certain intangible elements, and each person must live with the outcomes these elements produce.

At the positive extreme, these elements are servants to be commanded. At the negative extreme, they do the commanding. These slaves or masters of circumstance are called *life energy, intellect, and emotion*. Though various secular and religious philosophies refer to them differently, all agree that they exist and that they collaborate in a mind's development and function, and finally in the outcomes that a mind produces for its owner.

It is not their existence but their separation of functions that come into question. The terms selected here for examining these invisible forces fit today's language, allowing a framework inside of which to form a discussion.

Life Energy

A kernel of wheat has life energy but no intellect or emotion. Planted and cared for, a kernel of wheat replicates itself in new kernels of wheat, and its posterity may do so forever provided a continuation of proper soil fertility, heat, light, air, and moisture. In this sense, the life energy in a kernel of wheat is eternal, passing its vital power from one generation to the next forever.

Life energy in every multiplying organism, in every plant and animal species, has genetic memory encoded in DNA, one-half of the DNA code contributed by each parent. While this tiny recording keeps species pure of contamination from other species, it also contains the miraculous formula depended upon by life energy for the necessary chemistry to perpetuate this unseen eternal flame—the force that lights every cell within all living structures.

The higher up the food chain a species finds itself, the more minutia falls under DNA control. In humans and other advanced mammals, in addition to determining hair color, eye color, sex, and other physical traits, DNA even includes data specific to unique dispositional and intellectual traits.

The Intellect

The intellect is different from life energy. The intellect resides in the brain, expressing the personality, character, and acumen of a mind. The intellect is the source of logic, the foundation of the mind, and, in religious terms, the spirit of the soul.

In arriving at the myriad determinations that a mind must conclude every day, the intellect respects logic, and reasons through stored data, incoming sensual data, and data referred to as cosmic or spiritual data.[4][5] It then aggregates this data so that they can be measured against ethical,[6] moral,[7] and performance standards[8]. The intellect then emotes a feeling of either affirmation or dismissal, finally determining which way to go.

Scientifically determining an issue is different. In scientifically determining an issue, data being considered must satisfy the criteria of hardened fact, no emoting, and no waiting for social approval.

Presented to every intellect during earth's sojourn is an endless string of such determinations or choices.[9] An intellect advances when a right choice overcomes a difficult circumstance. Significant in this process, a higher standard for choice builds intellectual capacity—brainpower—faster than a lower standard. Since one's intellectual prowess will be no greater than the standards chosen to build it, judiciously selecting, and abiding by one's ethical, moral, and performance standards, becomes fundamental to personal progress. Why choose standards capable of less?

In a vital connection, every judgment and discovery that an intellect makes, from managing one's personal budget to discovering a cure for some insidious disease, happens most efficiently within an intellect minimally burdened with behavioral debris, debris avoided

---

4. Einstein and other notable discoverers speak of a cosmic religious feeling that accompanies meaningful discovery. Einstein: *"In my view, it is the most important function of art and of science to awaken this cosmic religious feeling and to keep it alive in those who are receptive to it."*

5. Dr. J.B. Rhine: *"That man possesses some 'extra sensory' factor [is] no longer doubted . . . telepathy, precognition, and clairvoyance have been established by scientific laboratory experiments . . . We have found that there is a capacity for acquiring knowledge that transcends the sensory functions. This extra-sensory capacity can give us knowledge certainly of objective and very likely of subjective states, knowledge of matter and most probably of minds."*

6. Ethics: Codes of conduct put forward by *outside* sources such as workplace rules or the principles of one's religious source.

7. Moral: One's *own* principles regarding right and wrong.

8. Performance: *Actual* behavior according to one's professed ethical and moral standards.

9. Reference book: Brian Abbey, *We Are the Choices We Make*

by an intellect choosing and abiding by high ethical, moral, and performance standards.

Emotion

While the intellect reasons through data, emotion coaxes that reasoning with feeling, feeling generally stimulated by the five senses and by the powerful compulsions of survival of the individual and reproduction of the species. Emotional output ranges all the way from a thunderbolt of hate powerful enough to encourage taking another's life to the tenderness of parental love.

Certainly, emotion fuels man's primal survival mechanism: the competitive drive. The competitive survival force civilly manifests itself in athletics, games generally, and not just keeping up with the Joneses but exceeding them. Reproduction's emotional spectrum spans the gulf between the deep reward of man and woman physically and emotionally bonded to one another, and thusly to the children, and sexual license's superficiality; sex's most profound result contrasted with shallow self-indulgence.

Emotion rewards the intellect when behaving worthily and batters the intellect when behaving unworthily. Emotions of delight, satisfaction, and joy, reward the intellect for an upright choice while emotions of guilt, regret, and depression, punish the intellect for a poor choice.

Emotion is the spice of accomplishment and the dejection of unmet hope. Emotion is ecstasy, agony, and all feeling in between. Thus, emotion signals the intellect to steer itself always toward its best result.

Intuition and Inspiration

Intuition and inspiration fill a special emotional category. Endless stories tell of an inspirational prompting suddenly occurring and changing history. Where do such promptings come from? How does one discern inspiration's source? Might a clean intellect intuitively discern direction better than a cluttered one?

Allegorically seeing the intellect—the mind—as a garden into which a seed planted inevitably yields its fruit, motivates an intellect to carefully choose the fruit seeded. As ye sow—or as ye allow to be sown—so shall you reap.[10]

---

10. Scripture: *"For they have sown the wind, and they shall reap the whirlwind."*

Chapter 2
A Work of Art

A forming human intellect is like a statue emerging from a block of marble, forever revealing itself beneath pecks of the hammer and chisel of experience. And experience results when one's ethical, moral, and performance standards collide with circumstance, forcing a choice.

The primary *goal* of the intellect is survival—and not just any survival but survival in an ever-improving circumstance.

The *power* of the intellect lies in its discretionary choice from among ethical, moral, and performance options, and executing upon the most refined determination it can make, and the determination can be no more refined than the standard by which it is measured.

The *glory* of the intellect is that it belongs to itself, to be mastered and enjoyed by itself, including those that depend on it and those with whom it associates.

Tender/Calloused

The effect of behavioral debris upon the intellect is not unlike the blind attempting to read Braille with hardened and calloused fingertips; it cannot be done well. The virtuous intellect—do not read weak, naïve, or dull—interprets purpose and design more efficiently than the promiscuous intellect. Intellectual debris such as guilt, regret, revenge, envy, slothfulness, and hatred, harden the intellect, making it difficult for purpose, design, and joy to get through.

Silent Thoughts

Finding itself constantly awash within the tumult of worldly survival, the intellect becomes not only its thoughts but a portion of what happens between its thoughts. Thought is deliberate intellectual stimulation and activation. During moments of intellectual silence, when purposeful thought lays silent, a mind migrates toward its environment. And the world's environment challenges the intellect with a daily—even hourly—obstacle course replete with psychological pathogens such as unending pornographic affronts, constant arrays of unwholesome foods and drugs, temptations of dishonesty, shameless civility, political deceit, unreconciled guilt, and vain imaginings, to name a few.

A wise man once said, *"A man is what he thinks about all day long."* Judiciously managing one's mental environment by eliminating the world's psychological noise keeps one's intellect clean, sharp, and efficient, fully able to *think all day long,* thus serving its owner at maximum capacity.

Moments of quiet, of purposefully blocking out worldly disturbance, of placing one's intellect, instead, within the nourishing environment of select reading, of refined music, of bright conversation, of directed meditation, and of prayer, requires planning and determination.

Intellectual Marvel

Fortunately, intellectual marvels happen. Albert Einstein is a favorite intellectual marvel, and upon his passing a wealth of information remains about his life.

Notable among Albert's many accomplishments, he employed an estimated 20% of brain matter in discovering through mathematical calculation the amount of atomic energy contained within a particle of matter: $E=mc^2$.

The average intellect utilizes about half that much gray matter and just manages to pay the rent. Whatever the difference between Albert's intellectual capacity and that of the average person, the observation remains that there is quite a leap of intellectual ability when, say, 20% of brain function comes into play compared to 10%.

Has it ever occurred to you how much energy a peanut would produce if all the atomic energy within each of its molecules were liberated? Clearly, Einstein did not see matter in the form of a peanut but wondered about the amount of atomic energy contained within a quantity of matter and discovered a formula for its calculation.

This example suggests that every project upon which mankind embarks begins in someone's mind as an intellectual spark, a thought, a wondering. All great accomplishments from vaccines against plagues to computer technology, from modern air travel to the finest musical compositions, owe their existence to some intellect taking a spark of wonder and creating a miracle.

Without question, the most notable and noble object to be created is the whole being, the complete person, the finest self, the comprehensive mind. If the mind is eternal as Judeo-Christianity states, and one can never escape one's mind, it makes sense to make one's mind accomplished and whole—to make it an entertaining place in which to dwell. Forever is a long time. A similar point can be made when holding a godless view of the human experience; even though the end is known, the journey might as well be worthwhile.

Energy/Intellect/Spirit

Einstein proved that matter and energy are just different versions of the same thing, like steam and water. Water acted upon by enough energy (heat) becomes steam. In Einstein's famous theory of relativity, energy and matter stand on opposite sides of the equal sign: $E=mc^2$.[11] Because the human spirit is energy, is it matter also?

God-based religion holds that the intellect is eternal matter, something real, something existing on its own. God-based religion also holds that an infant's intellect is not created in the same manner as the infant's life energy. This philosophy also holds that the intellect—the human mind—owes its origin to a divine source, making its arrival sometime between conception and birth, plausibly as soon as there is a vessel to hold it.

The further medical science delves into the womb, the earlier it appears that the intellect expresses itself within the fetus' developing body. Fetal response to outside stimuli happens within mere weeks of conception, prior even to nervous-system formation.

In regular anecdotal occurrence, a person—even a stranger to a recently impregnated woman—may sense the woman's pregnancy within days of her having conceived in her womb. Is this one intellect detecting the arrival of another?

Secularists view *life energy* and *intellect* as the same thing. Secularly, new life originates within the womb as an expansion of the parents' life, enjoying one-half its DNA code from each, like wheat. While DNA code does genetically connect child to parents, influencing the child physically and intellectually, it does not control the outcome of the child's life as it does in wheat. Wheat makes no choices; it only reacts to its environment.

The choices a child makes are ultimately self-derived, originating increasingly within the child's intellect as the child matures. The

---
11. $E=mc^2$: Energy equals mass times the speed of light squared.

intellect that is the child's true identity will at some point—most notably during teenage years—demonstrate this fact.

Though most childhood behavior mimics adult behavior, as knowledge increases within the child's intellect, the child raises its performance above that of its parents. This accounts for a portion of human progress over the centuries.

Pre-Programming

Judeo-Christianity holds that humankind's drive to improve circumstance comes pre-programmed into each intellect because each comes to earth formed in the intellectual image of its Creator, its literal spiritual Father. If the God of God-based religion is all that He is claimed to be, witnessing His management of the cosmos indicates that He has an intellect already developed to 100% capacity. How could He not?

Logically, then, if humankind has been formed in the Father's image, then where *He* is, that is where *His children* are programmed to arrive, and where they will arrive given sufficient time, information, self-discipline, and freedom in which to act. Infinity would be hell otherwise. And this is where America's founders radically departed from any known civilization ever to have existed on earth. They formed a government focused upon maximizing opportunity for each individual's personal progress by maximizing freedom—liberty. In fact, the Bill of Rights came about out of fear that government—as governments always do—would limit freedom, thereby limiting a citizen's opportunity for personal expression, personal growth, and personal progress.

Intellectual Growth Rate

Since America's founding, each decade has seen an increasing rate of technological advance. For example, a process that took ten years to develop in 1776, by 1876 may have taken only seven years, by 1976 only two years, and by 2020 only two months. This example suggests that the world's quantity of, and processing of, knowledge expands and has expanded geometrically. An intellect expands the same way; the more it expands its knowledge base, the *faster* it expands its knowledge base.

This creates a storage problem. What solves the problem of efficiently storing and recalling brain-stored information? Solving such a problem requires order, and the boundaries of *truth* are what bring order to mental chaos. Accurately recalling facts that have been stored within truth's definitive walls succeeds far better than trying to reassemble fiction. But assigning such a duty to *truth* poses a second problem: What is truth?

Lately, truth's implication has been tossed around so casually that its very meaning has become cloudy. New Age proponents often refer to one truth for you and another truth for someone else about the same subject. What? Why would the very word whose meaning is normally protected by impregnable walls have its meaning maneuvered?

So, what is truth? How does one discover truth and, once it's been found, remain within truth's protective walls?

Chapter 3
Objectivity – The Pathway to Truth and Clear Thinking

*I*magine that while walking along the beach one day you notice a bottle bobbing about in the surf. You pick it up and uncork it only to have a genie pop out, offering to grant you a single wish. What would that wish be? What single request would give you all that life can offer?

Would it be the world's largest oil well? Oil has great value and can be traded for many material possessions. But do material possessions fulfill all that life offers? They do not. There is only one commodity that fulfills all that life offers, and that commodity is truth.[12]

Truth matters. Truth is all that matters. Why? Because learning the truth about an issue leads toward mastery of that issue. Learning the truth about the stock market leads to wealth. Learning the truth about disease leads to prevention and cures. Learning the truth about geology can lead to oil and mineral discovery. Learning the truth about chemistry can lead to miracle compounds that facilitate life. Learning the truth about personal relationships allows love's consummation

---
12. Scripture: *"And ye shall know the truth, and the truth shall make you free."*

at the highest level, enhancing relations with one's spouse, children, family, trusted friends, and business associates.

Truth is intelligence.

Truth is absolute.

Truth is reality.

A notion unfounded in truth is just an empty thought, a hollow rationalization, vain imagining, fiction. Fiction imagines a voice. Truth is the voice. No single possession equates to truth, to finding truth, to implementing truth, and to harvesting truth's rewards.

Objectivity, Logic, and Solutions

Going back to ancient Greece, Aristotle placed the concept of *logic* at the very foundation of every inquiry, every argument, and every philosophical discussion, refusing to participate without its recognition. Since logic is defined as *valid reasoning*, it is not hard to understand why Aristotle and other notable philosophers demand(ed) logic as prerequisite to launching into meaningful discussion.

Why the demand for logic? Because logic-based reasoning compared to emotion-based reasoning—if emotion and reasoning can even be fitted into the same sentence—provides the greatest chance for a rational conclusion, for learning, and for progress.

Searching for logic among college curricula, one discovers that the concept of logic finds more anxious welcome in physical science than in liberal arts. Why is logic more welcome in physical science than in liberal arts? Logic is the absolute premise of physics, chemistry, computer science, and mathematics because each of these disciplines leads thought toward a finite conclusion, a definite answer, a number, a reality, a truth.

Liberal arts does not find that same constraint. The emotive nature of paintings, theater, movies, sculpture, poetry, prose, philosophy, music, history with its innumerable rewrites, and language itself, have as many emotional effects upon the observer as there are subjects to observe.

Logic's properties are 1) <u>Consistency</u>: no theorem of a logical system contradicts another; 2) <u>Validity</u>: logical thought only uses premises that prove factual—true; 3) <u>Completeness</u>: if a formula is true, it can be proven, and; 4) <u>Soundness</u>: arguments that are true in the actual world—not the hypothetical world—are logical.

Notice that three of logic's four premises are defined by truth. Aristotle's demand for logic equates to a demand for the objectivity that only truth provides. The American Mind seeks no less. Using America's political divide as an example: What is the best way to approach America's race mixture, America's economy, or America's military attitude? Three things must be present to reconcile fractured opinions about such topics: 1) People discussing or debating these issues must be of good will, willing to start from scratch, setting aside prior potentially prejudicial opinions; 2) People must agree that objective reality exists and that discovering the objective reality of an issue leads to its best approach or solution; and 3) People must be willing to change their views as facts are determined.

The politician rarely solves these issues; rather, the politician inflames them to rev up his voter base.[13] But, in spite of political maneuvering, America's societal advance lies in the American Mind's determined course. Think of the American Mind's revolt against slavery's injustice, sacrificing its own blood to eliminate it. Think of the American Mind's revolt against global totalitarianism and expending its own blood and treasure to eliminate it as well. Think of Native Americans' harsh treatment by early generations, repaired as best could be accomplished by later generations.

---

13. When asked in a 2008 presidential debate what criteria each candidate would use to select a Supreme Court justice, McCain responded, paraphrasing, *"A nominee with a history of following the Constitution."* Obama responded, *"One that would stand up for a struggling single mother."* McCain was objective. Obama was subjective. In seeking justice, law (the Constitution) has objectively defined parameters. In subjectivity, law is blown about by winds of opinion.

Personal Objectivity

A person willing to pay the price finds that the reward of objectivity far outweighs the cost of acquiring this distinctiveness. To maximize personal progress, one must recognize that objective reality encompasses every topic on earth. With the acceptance of this point comes unmatched intellectual distinction.

Why is the cost of objectivity so high? The cost is high because personal progress is the point, and when one compares the ease of concocted rationalization to the harshness of objective evaluation, ease holds great sway.

Objectivity turns the intellect to introspection, to strict accountability, and away from easy excuses and hollow rationalizations. Facing and correcting shortfalls is not an easy-come-easy-go process. Because of its difficult nature, every time one conquers a shortfall or overcomes weakness or temptation by holding to objective ethical, moral, and performance standards, each triumph adds its portion to willpower. Soon to appear alongside mounting willpower is its worthy companion: self-confidence. And personal triumph, appearing however remote in the moment, awaits upon the same path.

Applied to science, sociology, politics, education, religion, or any other subject, the same holds true: As facts that challenge long held beliefs emerge, changing one's mind to embrace objective reality can be difficult; liberating but difficult.

Objectivity and Equality

Since no two human lives enjoy equal portions of life's talents, inputs, efforts, and resources, no life outcome is, can be, or will be equal to any other. Critical here is that all lives experience social justice so long as the law is equally applied. This is social justice in its objective form, and life's varied outcomes cannot be overcome by some vote-seeker promising to provide social justice in the form of equal

Chapter 3 * Objectivity – The Pathway to Truth and Clear Thinking

outcomes. Such is the basis for socialism, and such is why socialism fails. Placing the American Mind in this socialist construct is to place it in a cage, disallowing its rise, a constraint it cannot and will not accept. Taking socialism to its natural conclusion, upward mobility disappears when everyone must end at the same finish line; everyone except the politician.[14]

To promise equal outcomes as social justice is dishonest, cruel, and overtly stupid. Put into action, this counterfeit for justice must forcibly confiscate property and opportunity from high performers to be redistributed to lower performers. How socially just is that? Without objectivity, humanity and human behavior become subjects of opinion, paving the way for bias and prejudice.[15][16]

In objectivity, reward is commensurate with productivity. In subjectivity, reward becomes the gift of opinion, and the individual, however earnest, dedicated, or nobly applied, is denied the full production of his efforts. Witness America's race industry. Witness cries about income inequality and how socialism will fix it. Witness India's social castes, most African societies, and Muslim-dominated societies relegating the feminine half of their population to obscurity, servitude, and social restriction.

Further, by pushing the notion that income inequality is unjust, the politician that is either corrupt or stupid or both, subjectively turns the economic non-performer against the performer, against the same economic performer that supports the economy that feeds and houses the performer and the non-performer, including the politician. Furthermore, American political subjectivity promotes certain citizens

---

14. When the Soviet Union collapsed, soviet citizens were appalled to see the luxuriousness of the lives that their politicians had been living. Surprised, anyone?

15. Please refer to footnote 13, the McCain and Obama debate.

16. By substituting the word 'equity' for the word 'equality', Leftist ideology supports the notion that all must end at the same place in life regardless. High performers must be brought low not to shame lower performers. This is fake justice, and human nature revolts at such fakeness.

over others in education and the workplace. American political subjectivity taxes a greater percentage of money from high-performing citizens than from lesser performers, and no tax at all from most. Such subjectivity disconnects the non-paying citizen from one of life's vital realities: life's cost in terms of effort.

Subjectivity allows political correctness to restrict discussion of social concerns, concerns that if discussed objectively would expose, clarify, and improve unproductive social trends. Subjectivity differentiates between abortion at six weeks from conception and abortion at nine months from conception; an unborn human life taken is still a human life taken. Political subjectivity gives impunity to one who lies about a topic like sex. How does reclassifying a lie make it not a lie?

Objectivity and Reality

The ability of a human mind to objectively assess reality and to act upon reality outpaces every known method for advancing life. Reality is truth, and reality cannot and will not tolerate a lie. Reality eventually tracks down every lie and exposes not only the lie but its fabricator as well. Everyone who has challenged reality with even the slightest falsehood has learned, or will learn, that reality does an excellent job of keeping life, including science, between the lines.

A popular tool for manipulating reality—objectivity—is to change the meaning of words. While there are many examples, these few stand out: actress, marriage, supremacy, trans-, and diversity.

Actress: Every noun has assigned gender. Many languages are gender-based in construct and pronunciation. In the English case, actor is male; actress is female. Calling an actress an actor supports the notion of a genderless world, denying the beauty, structure, and reality of nature itself. Why do something so demonstrably fake? How tragic must a figure be to require fake support?

Marriage: Marriage is one of Christendom's seven sacramental pillars.[17] To the Christian the word *marriage* is a sacramental notation defining the God-ordained eternal binding of man and woman, civilization's foundation unit; destroy the foundation and the house crumbles.[18] God profoundly sanctions this union on behalf of the tender little ones that follow, and on behalf of all society. What word must the Christian now use to mean what the word *marriage* used to mean? Is the new term *holy matrimony*?[19]

Supremacy: When did a disciplined life become supremacy? When did education and a strong work ethic become supremacy? When did sex within wedlock become supremacy? When did holding the family unit together on behalf of the children become supremacy? When did a two-parent household become supremacy? When did launching one generation from upon the shoulders of the previous one become supremacy?

---

17. The Seven Christian Sacraments:
    1. Baptism: The act of spiritual rebirth, exiting the baptismal water as Jesus did, one now becomes His covenanted and cleansed disciple.
    2. Confirmation: Authorized clergy confirm a newly baptized person a member of the congregation of Jesus Christ.
    3. Sacrament of the Last Supper (Eucharist): At His Last Supper, Jesus commanded that his disciples regularly partake of consecrated wine (water commonly substituted) to represent His sacrificial blood and bread to represent his sacrificial flesh, martyred on humanity's behalf.
    4. Repentance: Feeling remorse for a misdeed and putting away unproductive behavior in favor of a new start, at the same time doing all possible to make whole anyone caught in the misdeed.
    5. Anointing: Applying a drop of consecrated oil to the sick and suffering accompanied by a blessing of healing. Also, bestowal of religious authority.
    6. Marriage: The holy binding of man and woman for all time, sanctified by God on behalf of the couple and the children that follow—society's bedrock civil unit.
    7. Ordination: Setting individuals apart by authorized clergy to serve in holy capacities such as teachers, ministers, priests, and others that administer to fellow man's spiritual needs.

18. Scripture *"We warn that the disintegration of the family will bring upon individuals, communities, and nations the calamities foretold by ancient and modern prophets."*

19. Obergefell v. Hodges: When asked by Justice Scalia if a civil union with every legal protection provided bisexual couples would suffice, the plaintiffs demanded the word itself: *marriage*.

Trans-: Transition means to change from one state to another. DNA does not transition.

Diversity: When was the word *diversity* restricted only to ethnicity or gender? When was diversity disallowed in terms of differing opinions or political or religious philosophies?

Objectivity and Law

From her beginning, America's success can be attributed to the grasp of objectivity noted in her founding. As a founding governmental document, the U.S. Constitution is recognized as the most objective basis for civil law ever devised in world history.

America's founders reinforced their concept of objective governance with a vital support: They conceived the Supreme Court with its mission of objective vigilance of constitutional alignment in evolving law. Why the need for objective legal backup from the Court? Because objective governance, governance untainted by shifting public opinion, provides equal and sustainable liberty to each citizen, allowing each citizen and minority group to choose a standard of behavior and to follow that standard to its promised conclusion.

Should law become subjective, allowing legal premise to shift in one political philosophy's direction, what happens to the rights of those of a differing opinion? That is why the American Mind gives objective law such acclaim and defends its product of *equality before the law* so vigorously.

In an environment of objective law one's upward rise depends upon one's ethics and performance and not upon someone's opinion of one's ideals. Specifically, the higher the ethical, moral, and performance standards one adopts, the more productive one becomes, and the more productive one becomes, the greater the reward to be realized in an improving circumstance.

Chapter 3 * Objectivity – The Pathway to Truth and Clear Thinking

Objectivity and Justice

Abiding objectivity is difficult at first because objectivity demands justice. While objectivity *demands* justice, subjectivity *inherits* justice. In like manner, the objective person expects, demands, and depends upon justice, logically, because, as subjectivity shoots at a moving target, objectivity aims at a predictable reward, and reward improves circumstance. Life's purpose on any other basis drifts. But how does objectivity demand justice while subjectivity inherits justice?

Sir Isaac Newton described one of justice's physical components in his third law of motion: *For every action, there is an equal and opposite reaction.* Or, for the exertion of force in any direction, there is an opposing force in the opposite direction of the same magnitude. The two forces balance one another in physical justice; they justify each other.

In human action—action based upon belief as all human action is—there are two types of consequences that, added together, justify the belief that prompts the action. These two types of consequences are intended consequence and unintended consequence. Added together, intended and unintended consequences justify the belief that sponsored the action; they sort out and expose the belief's founding premise, proving or disproving its worth.

Should a fellow who believes the earth to be flat be called upon to design the flightpath of a satellite, one would hope that the word *orbit* might cause a moment's pause. A fellow who believes that he must answer traffic insults by ramming offending cars with his own will encounter consequences of another sort: While the intent of his belief would be to administer revenge as justice, real justice will be answered in every unintended traffic tie-up caused by his revenge; every unintended change of insurance companies and soaring premium costs; every unintended time the rammed motorist sued him; and the unintended influence of his dark method in all aspects of his life.

So long as there is equality before the law, justice will prevail—particularly social justice. One may choose one's actions but not the consequences—not the justice.

Objectivity and Reward

It happens that the more objective a belief is, the greater the likelihood of justice as a *reward* for following that belief rather than justice as a *penalty* for following it. Consider *choice*, *justice*, and *reward and penalty*. Everyone makes *choices*. Every *choice* results in *justice*, and *justice* will either *reward* or *penalize*.

Objectivity and Skill

Inseparably connected to objective belief, and among its greatest compensations, is the principle that the farther down the ladder one begins, and the more difficult the climb, the greater the skill developed in the ascent. Robbing one of the opportunity to overcome one's challenges robs one of the skills acquired in overcoming, and these skills happen to be the very ones lacking in the first place—the ones always missing at the bottom and only identifiable and attainable in the ascent.

These are proficiencies that cannot be granted nor gifted. By their nature, they must be earned before they can be understood and implemented, much less owned. Of what reliability is a gifted plateau supported by thin air?

Skill, self-discipline, self-confidence, and personal empowerment come quickly to a mind thusly embarked, along with the reliable qualities of steadfastness and focus, of an unfailing work ethic, of fidelity to such standards as honesty and virtue, and a willingness to sacrifice the moment for something better in the future.

That is why America's founders established objective, not arbitrary or subjective law, and stopped there. Law that objectively provides each citizen with peace, liberty, and the protection of property[20] was their ideal. The rest would be up to the citizen—make of himself what he would; pursue happiness as he would; seek spiritual and material prosperity as he would. And that is where belief in character—the focus, strength, and nobility of the inner person—comes to bear.

True to the scale of the project or attempt, subjectivity is inherently flawed as a basis for analysis, planning, and action while objectivity aligns with logic, reason, constancy, honesty, intelligence, and reward.[21]

Justice and Mercy

It no doubt occurred to you while studying objectivity that mercy mitigates justice, and that mercy is subjective. This is true. But in its intended administration, mercy remains a gift from one to another. Mercy cannot be self-administered.[22] Self-administration corrupts mercy into self-indulgence, self-pity, and rationalization, all paths to nowhere.

---

20. John Locke (1632–1704): The British social philosopher and political writer from whom Jefferson gathered much of the Declaration of Independence's content, listed the goals of government to be the protection of life, liberty, and property. Jefferson softened Locke, listing instead life, liberty, and the pursuit of happiness. The pursuit of happiness is subjective and a poor substitute for property. Property cannot be as easily converted to subjective interpretation as can the vague concept of *happiness*.

21. Positioned for failure are subjective substitutions of ethnicity or gender for intelligence, talent, and skill via identity politics.

22. Are drug addicts and alcoholics keen enough about treating their own distresses to *self-medicate*?

Section 2
Moral, Rational, and Good and Bad

Rarely acknowledged yet most constructive among all intellectual disciplines is that of *moral agency*. Why haven't you heard of *moral agency* until now? You haven't heard of *moral agency* until now because it ranks among the most difficult of intellectual distinctions; and only the most determined soul dares to embrace it. But, as always, exceptional effort begets exceptional results, which in the case of *moral agency* represents a rising American Mind.

In addition to introducing *moral agency*, this section explains a second and equally powerful concept: *rational self-interest*. Identified over two-hundred years ago, the invention of the United States of America spawned a self-interested population that took civilization to heights never imagined in world history much less accomplished. What possible behavioral formula expanded self-interest to mutual interest—that by one person lifting himself causes those about him to rise as well?

This section closes by exploring the eternal opposites: *good* and *bad*. It identifies how the American Mind qualifies each and how it navigates the two.

Chapter 4
Moral Agency

*F*inding truth through objective search ranks among the most remunerative intellectual techniques that a human mind can possess. But finding truth is only the beginning: To realize its value, truth must be acted upon; truth must be pointed in a productive direction. Why leave any intellectual force to wander undirected through one's mind, much less a force with the potential to improve one's life to the degree that truth does?

As the compass force upon which it would rely for pointing truth in its most productive direction, the American Mind turns to *moral agency*. Why? Because *moral agency* mandates that an intellect follow a higher path as soon as it is recognized or recognizable. *Moral agency* is an intellect's virtuous initiative. *Moral agency* is the demand of a proactive conscience. *Moral agency* obliges an intellect to choose what is right, to choose what is best, and to choose what is true. *Moral agency* happens within an intellect for whom personal progress—improving oneself and one's circumstance—is the point.

Easily confused with moral agency is the concept of *free agency*, sometimes called *free will*. While the difference between terms is little, the difference between the concepts is great. Free agency and free will intimate that an intellect may choose any act it pleases at any time it pleases. But for an intellect settled upon selected ethical, moral, and performance standards, that intellect is no longer free to act any way it pleases. It now becomes *morally obligated* to follow its selected standards as part of future behavior.

For example, consider a Christian confronted with the prospect of telling a lie. Once acceding to the Christian imperative for honest personal conduct, the Christian individual becomes *morally bound* to truthfulness. Honesty now becomes a *moral imperative*, and the Christian intellect, acting as a *moral agent unto itself*, must demonstrate honest personal conduct. Should honesty not prevail in a Christian's behavior, labels of hypocrite and/or apostate apply.

Moral Agency and Intellectual Freedom and Safety

Along with an intellect's never-ending quest for truth, immunizing that intellect against life's myriad intellectual pathogens becomes a significant step. This is done by selecting a strong code of conduct and upholding it. How can seeking out and upholding a strong code of conduct not be meaningful to one's life?

Some people believe that following a particular behavioral code, especially one put forward by someone other than themselves, including one reportedly put forward by God, restricts personal freedom when exactly the opposite happens. It is naïve to assume that freeing the intellect from predetermined behavioral standards keeps it free from all else. In the absence of standards selected precisely for their influence upon personal development, the world imposes its standards instead. And the world's standards are quick to replace choice with compulsion, thus jeopardizing personal progress.[23] [24]

---

23. C.S. Lewis: *"There are two kinds of people: those who say to God, 'Thy will be done,' and those to whom God says, 'All right, then; have it your way.'"*

24. Yogi Berra: *"If you don't know where you're going, you might wind up someplace else."*

Certain of life's attractions bind the intellect. Binding the intellect threatens personal progress. Think of addiction. Think of drug abuse. Think of sexual promiscuity and its aftermaths of treachery, lechery, lost hope, exploitation, filth, disease, rejection, loneliness, and guilt. Examples beyond the limitations of drugs and sex include addictions to unhealthy food, slothfulness, dishonesty, unnecessary debt, and wasted time.

No greater intellectual freedom exists than that resulting from applying moral agency to the most refined behavioral code one can discover. No action one can take better assures joyful living.

Standards, Choice, and Freedom

For an intellect to strengthen maximally, it must be free to pit chosen behavioral standards against conflicting options as they present themselves. This is the American Mind's imperative for freedom. Unless an intellect is free to choose the right as its standards dictate, and then act, it remains stifled, restricted and imprisoned, caged like an animal. Thus, the American Mind's early maxim: *"Give me liberty or give me death!"*

It is only by having sufficient freedom in which to choose between good, better, and best—by proactively overcoming oneself—that strength of character accumulates; individual character, familial character, and societal character. The fullest realization of self only occurs in this manner.

The growth of a mind that holds behavior within select standards outdistances a mind either forced to obey a behavioral standard—Sharia Law, Socialism, or Communism—or one absent any standard at all. In choosing its behavioral standard, the original American Mind chose the most difficult behavioral standard known at the time or since: Judeo-Christian doctrine.

In choosing Judeo-Christianity as its ethical, moral, and performance standard, the American Mind became a moral agent unto itself, bound by Judeo-Christian moral, ethical, and performance standards—standards so refined that they created a mind fit enough for the first time on earth to self-govern[25].

With no sovereign to lord over it, no politic to dictate its daily schedule, no forced religious homage, and no social caste that held it prisoner, Judeo-Christian moral agency launched the American Mind into realms of civic, scientific, economic, and moral heights previously unimagined in the human experience.

Moral Agency, Law, and Results

The U.S. Constitution's unleashing of the Judeo-Christian behavioral code within a society of unimagined freedom brought upon the world a burst of economic and technological advance unknown and unimagined even by the very men who wrote it. Why did that happen, and why does it continue to happen?

As noted, second to survival no known internal directive exceeds the human mind's desire to move up in the world, to improve its circumstance, to succeed on behalf of self and family. Witness the queue of foreigners willing to risk even death to come to America.

America is attractive to those outside her borders because America's people appear free to answer mankind's universal desire for personal progress. Because of this perception, America may appear a magical place, but it is not. Not always seen from afar but essential to America's success are the ethical, moral, and performance criteria by which that upward mobility is facilitated, and by which it is

---

25. Theodore Roosevelt: *"Self-government is not an easy thing. Only those communities are fit for it in which the average individual practices the virtues of self-command, of self-restraint, of self-disinterestedness [unselfishness]. It is no light task for a nation to achieve the temperamental qualities without which the institutions of free government are but an empty mockery. Our people are now successfully governing themselves, because for more than a thousand years they have been slowly fitting themselves [adopting Judeo-Christian ethical, moral, and performance standards], sometimes consciously, sometimes unconsciously, toward this end."*

maintained. America is a place pragmatically rooted in, and dependent upon, her people's love of, and adherence to, Judeo-Christianity's powerful history of ethical, moral, and performance success. And this is where the argument between *free agency* and *moral agency* heats up.

He that professes *free agency* resents moral obligation getting in the way of his choices and methods. He feels that he must be free to seek life's pursuits by whatever means. *The moral agent*, on the other hand, following select ethical, moral, and performance standards, seeks life's pursuits within guidelines proven to assure a predictable outcome.

The two-sided coin of personal agency—*moral agency* obliging one to choose the moral right and *free agency* suggesting freedom to make any choice—lies at the heart of America's political divide. Because of the gulf between these two methods, debate about the two rages on in political ideology and theory. It always has and it always will. Good and evil do exist. Good, better, and best, also exist. One is free to choose how one will travel one's path.

Chapter 5
Adam Smith and Rational Self-Interest

A quiet historical coincidence happened in America's special year of 1776. Scottish social philosopher and pioneer economist, Adam Smith (1720–1790), published *An Inquiry into the Nature and Causes of the Wealth of Nations*. Among the many novel concepts that Smith described in his economic exposé is that of *rational self-interest*—an often neglected element inherent in prosperity's equation.

Smith perceived a correlation between an individual's moral behavior and his economic success. He described how seeking self-interest within a set of *moral obligations* leads to prosperity. He explained how placing enough thusly motivated individuals within a free and competitive economic framework would produce an affluent civilization. He was not theorizing.

His proposed affluent civilization already existed in Pennsylvania. He had visited Quaker Pennsylvania and had investigated its economic system. He had witnessed its potential. Without the coinciding formation of the United States, Smith's view would have taken more time to prove itself, if ever it would.²⁶ The Declaration of Independence changed all that. Putting rational self-interest, freedom, and economic competition into immediate and wholesale practice, America at once proved, and continues to prove, Smith's theory to be true.

Smith's view of *self-interest wrapped within a moral framework* defined the American Mind as it was coming into being. Consider Benjamin Franklin's query made toward the end of his life: *"How does one live a life that is useful, virtuous, worthy, moral, and spiritually meaningful?"*

Smith's theory of *rational self-interest* spoke to man's desire to do the best possible in his own interest, a natural tendency and goal. What made virtue out of this seemingly egotistical vice was the American Mind's ability to confine behavior within the *moral obligation* or *moral discipline* of Judeo-Christian ethics.

Releasing this moral personality within a highly competitive free-market system—capitalism—soon produced the economic athlete that the American Mind became and remains. Without doubt, the bombing of Pearl Harbor by the Japanese in 1941, the Muslim attack upon the World Trade Center in 2001, and today's internal Leftist attacks upon America's traditional business methods, represent belligerence against this mind; easier to kill it or cancel it than to take it on in toe-to-toe free-market competition.

---

26. Going as far back as 1723, before America's birth as a nation, Pennsylvania's local economy began with the local government's issuance of paper currency, a slip of paper legalized as *"tender"* for trade value. Since the borrower was a member of the citizenry that supported the government, should he take out a loan, he was, in effect, borrowing from fellow citizens, and the value of his trade medium—his slip of paper currency—depended upon his moral obligation to repay the loan. Should he default on his debt, that chunk of the local economy would disappear, and the totality of the local economy would be devalued by his defaulted portion. Conversely, applying his loan to a new business expanded the local economy. Did personal morality enter this equation? Did the individual become a *moral agent* in business matters? List the number of countries about the globe where a citizen can drive a car off the showroom floor with offering only a slight down payment. Credit fails without a moral citizenry. Can a person's credit rating also be a statement of that person's morality?

Virtue or Vice

Seeking self-interest outside moral framework leads to lechery, exploitation, and even crime. Seeking self-interest within moral framework spurs personal and familial progress, upward mobility, social and economic success, and advances in education, business, medical and technological science, and the arts. But this presents a problem for certain personalities.

For government to depend upon its citizenry to follow rational self-interest rather than strict governmental oversight, as governments are accustomed, gives citizenry extreme freedom, extreme enough that wild things can happen. But without extreme freedom, extreme opportunity cannot happen. Without extreme opportunity, extreme progress cannot happen. What, then, differentiates an heir of this demand for extreme freedom from other Americans? While the exact number of Americans possessing this attitude is unknowable, a quantitative analysis includes the following:

During the tumultuous decades of the 1770s and 1780s when America was separating herself from the United Kingdom, the colonial population divided itself into three political categories. Those with strong loyalty to the Crown formed the first group: Loyalists. A clear distinction separated Loyalists from the two remaining rebel groups.

Throughout America's Revolutionary War, and for years thereafter, Loyalists left what was becoming the United States. They left out of a sense of loyalty to their monarch, King George, and his United Kingdom. Though rough estimates exist as high as one-third of the total population, the exact number of colonials who either returned to England or migrated north to Canada is unknown.

Whether returning to England to build their fortunes anew or whether forging on to chilly Canada, Loyalists sought safe refuge under the Crown's protection. Safe refuge inherits reduced risk. With reduced risk comes reduced freedom and restricted opportunity.[27] Leading all categories of civil structure prized by the Rebels, extreme freedom (extreme by contemporary standards) and limitless opportunity—answerable self-interest—were liberties that neither group of American rebels would give up. Again, a single rallying cry encapsulates these sentiments: *"Give me liberty or give me death!"*[28]

Two Rebel Views

Not so clear a distinction as that between Loyalists and Rebels separated the two groups remaining in the colonies. Though united against the Crown in a war of separation, the two rebel groups afterward exhibited polar perspectives, especially when the time came to formulate law.

The rebel group to the right generally identified with founding father Alexander Hamilton. This group presented an aggressively commercial front, one fixed upon business and large enterprise, seeing great societal progress in the profit motive; avowed capitalists all.[29]

Inherent in this view, and most objectionable to the second group, was the centralization of governmental and financial power, and especially the combination of the two. Power sufficiently aggregated to

---

27. See Socialism, Communism, Sharia Law, and the American Left's political ideology.

28. Patrick Henry (1736-1799) Quotation from Henry's speech made to the Virginia Convention at St. John's Church in Richmond, Virginia, March 23, 1775, a speech credited with swinging the vote of the House of Burgesses in favor of fighting the British for independence. Henry: *"Is life so dear, or peace so sweet, as to be purchased at the price of chains and slavery? Forbid it, Almighty God! I know not what course others may take; but as for me, give me liberty or give me death!"*

29. Free-market capitalism: An economic system wherein capital, held by private citizens, is shifted by those citizens from areas of lesser productivity to those of greater productivity, thereby increasing competition and narrowing the profit margin that attracted capital to the more productive areas in the first place. As an example, in 1930, the average American family's food budget amounted to 25% of income. Today, owing precisely to private ownership of capital and the fierce competition among capitalist farmers, capitalist food processors, and capitalist retailers, food for a family today costs 7–9% of net family income, the lowest anywhere in the world. A similar curve happens in each commodity presented within a capitalist consumer economy. The first flat-screen television set sold for about $10,000 and today cost about $400. This explains U.S. world domination in terms of GDP and standard of living.

underpin the Hamiltonian mercantile plan was viewed as the imposition of unrighteous dominion by government upon the individual.

But without the new nation's wealth being centrally focused, no established foreign power could be enticed to make loans or enter into commercial contracts. How could such transactions be efficiently secured among innumerable and separate entities?

The group of rebels objecting to Hamilton's plan, the third group in this analysis, aligned with Thomas Jefferson's and Patrick Henry's view. This group resented and feared authority and was willing to die in the cause of ridding authority altogether. They not only sought riddance of the Crown, but any form of government telling an individual what to do with the product of his labor.

This group desired the most basic of freedoms; to simply be left to one's own appeals to logic and reason and not be swept up in any grand scheme that might compel a certain behavior or obligation not of one's choosing.

Each rebel side distrusted the other from the outset, and still does. Animosity between the two surfaced vividly in the Constitution's drafting and greatly complicated the document's ratification. This bitterness soon came to defeat John Adam's presidency and indirectly led to Aaron Burr's killing of Alexander Hamilton a few decades later. So which view is right?

American Distinctions

As these antagonistic ideologies morphed over the decades, they settled into political parties. These parties organized under a variety of names. They have been known as Whig, Federalist, Know-Nothings, the Fusion and People's Parties, Free-Soil and Anti-Nebraska, Greenback, Populist, American and Bull Moose, Independent, Libertarian, Constitutionalist, National, Green, Peace, Communist, Socialist, Democrat, Republican as progressive (anti-slavery) and

Republican as conservative (strict Constitutionalist), and more.

While these names suggest many distinctions, only two distinctions exist. America's never-ending debate is rooted in each. Political differences between individual Americans are rooted in each.

The first distinction struggles between *freedom* and *license*. Abraham Lincoln put it this way: *"We all declare for liberty (freedom); but in using the same word, we do not all mean the same thing. With some, the word liberty may mean for each man to do as he pleases with himself, and the product of his labor; while with others, the same word may mean for some men to do as they please with other men and the product of other men's labor. Here are two, not only different, but incompatible things, called by the same name—liberty. And it follows that each of the things is, by the respective parties, called by two different and incompatible names—liberty and tyranny."*

The second distinction arises in identifying and defining Smith's *moral obligation*. Smith could only have meant moral obligation to be the guiding force of individual conscience—moral agency—coming to bear when choice pits circumstance against a person's ethical, moral, and performance standards. No standard for personal conduct existed in Scotland or in America in the 1700s for Adam Smith to compare except those embodied within Judeo-Christian doctrine as it was strengthening immediately around him and on the other side of the Atlantic as well.[30]

Hamilton versus Jefferson

Examining the distinctions between Hamiltonian and Jeffersonian perspectives, the Hamiltonian request for centralized power gives

---

30. Smith's concept of *moral obligation* breaks down when someone not wishing to uphold a God-derived moral obligation still wants to uphold some other *moral obligation*. To champion a just cause, then, would make someone a *good person* despite personal conduct. Many accomplish this switch by crying out about income inequality or social injustice, rain forest devastation, cruelty to animals, or climate change. While these may be causes worth considering, their advocacy does not qualify character.

government broad authority—broad enough to influence a nation's entire economic structure and status.

A positive example of this power would be the concept of credit—borrowing and lending. Leveraging equity with a loan expands an economy much faster than waiting for equity to build. Thus, Hamilton's process expanded, and expands, the American economy at an alarming rate.

But leveraging inherits risk. Without borrowers' *moral obligation* minimizing the risk of leveraging, great tragedies happen such as the Great Depression, the savings and loan debacle, and the 2008 subprime, government-initiated[31] Wall Street debacle.

Jeffersonian ideology fears the yielding of independence to concentrated power. It resists being compelled to bow to economic authority, to civil authority, and to religious authority. The positive example of Jeffersonian independence is individual liberty—freedom to choose—to make choices that propel one upward and onward at one's chosen speed, unencumbered by forced behavior.[32]

But without consulting a *moral obligation* when confronting individual choice, unbridled freedom becomes license. On a national level, license derails order, resulting in the chaos of civil disobedience, economic instability, and tyrannical governmental imposition.[33]

Settled upon the individual life, license leads to poor choices in personal career and financial management, slothfulness and dishonesty (including infidelity), lying, and general deceit. Also included in

---

31. The Affordable Housing Act and its effect upon Fannie Mae's and Freddy Mac's lending policies, promoted by Democrat Representative Barney Frank and Democrat Senator Chris Dodd, led directly to the 2008 economic collapse. Wall Street simply took the money-making tool Frank and Dodd gave them, ran with it, and were quickly blamed by Frank, Dodd, and their political cronies for the mayhem that followed. Congress then began regulating Wall Street to keep them from ever doing this again by way of the Sarbanes-Oxley Act. How much sense does this make?

32. The Affordable Care Act is governmental will—personal mandate—forcefully imposed; comply or have your assets confiscated by government forces.

33. Governmental action like the Affordable Housing Act and the Affordable Care Act each mandated compliance by force.

license are the indulgences of divorce in spite of the children, abortion in spite of killing an unborn child, pornography in spite of harming the viewer, drug use and abuse rather than clear thinking, moral relativism rather than moral absolutes, and so on.

At every turn, evidence indicates that Hamiltonian economics has expanded the U.S. economy with more vigor, speed, and power than it could have expanded otherwise. In spite of its excesses, no other economy on the globe can keep up.[34]

Hamilton's plan brought prosperity into millions of homes not only in the United States but within homes of trading partners like Canada, Mexico, Germany, England, and Pacific Rim nations.

Would the Hamiltonian system have rung the financial alarm as often as it has if its employers had observed economic *moral obligations*, even individual *moral obligations*? Would Jefferson's unbridled freedom have led to today's twisted excesses in personal license if the highest known code for *personal moral conduct* guided individual choice?

---
34. GDP IMF 2019

Rank	Country/Territory	GDP (US $million)
	World	80,501,413
1	United States	19,485,394
2	China[n 5]	12,234,781
3	Japan	4,872,415
4	Germany	3,693,204
5	United Kingdom	2,631,228
6	France	2,582,492
7	India	2,575,666
8	Brazil	2,055,512
9	Italy	1,943,835
10	Canada	1,647,120

Rational/Logical/Moral/Personal

Adam Smith's use of the word *rational* in his phrase '*rational self-interest*' descends from concepts of logic and reason. With America's founding, the logic and reason that were to guide self-interest found embodiment within distinct ethics outlined within Judeo-Christian doctrine and, most profoundly, within Protestant Judeo-Christian doctrine.[35] Without Judeo-Christian doctrine as his basis for *rationality*, Scotsman Smith's theory would not have been possible.[36]

Unmatched in its ability to drive personal progress, the Judeo-Christian ethic stands alone and apart among all core values witnessed around the globe. The acute issue surrounding the success of this code in terms of national prosperity becomes not simply its powerful content, but finding enough of the population observing its intricacies to carry those who do not.

When Judeo-Christianity's ethical instruction becomes one's rationale for personal conduct, advancing one's character becomes a real and immediate process. Imagine the results when a mind applies Judeo-Christian standards to such personal issues as fidelity in marriage; managing one's personal economy; sexual propriety, including gender qualification; drug usage; and honest and charitable association with family, friends, neighbors, and business connections. How about extending their employ to issues like the responsibility of a Wall Street broker to client over self; that of a politician to country over self; especially that of a parent to child over self? Such behavior distinguishes the American Mind.

---

35. Average worker productivity in Protestant nations is 40% higher than in non-Protestant nations.

36. Recall that Smith had visited Quaker Pennsylvania and saw firsthand Judeo-Christianity's influence on personal conduct. Recall, too, that few denominations exceeded Quakers in applying Judeo-Christian ethics to civic conduct.

Section 3
Belief and the American Mind

One bases one's actions upon one's beliefs. Since one's actions can and will take one's life to any number of places, how and where belief is found matters. Following the American Mind's beliefs across the decades, the American Mind has taken itself to all sorts of places. One example is spending billions of dollars to help crush Nazi[37] Germany and then immediately spending billions more to rebuild the same country. Where did the beliefs come from that would lead a nation to do something like that? How did Russia's beliefs direct its post-war attitude toward Germany? A wall to keep people in, anyone?

While the family setting incubates belief within a child's emerging intellect, God-based and non-God-based religions and public and private education also play their parts, and so do media and peers. So, what should one make of belief's source? How is such a thing valued or measured? Is there a superior belief? If there is, what is it and what proves it so?

---

37. NAZI: Acronym for: National Socialist German Workers' Party

Section 3
Belief and the American Mind

Chapter 6
Belief's Consequences

One encounters beliefs held by the American Mind in many places, but nowhere is the subtlety of those beliefs on display more openly than in the Olympic Games.

During the opening ceremony of the 1936 Berlin Olympic Games, the American team startled attending nations. As over five-thousand athletes from fifty-one nations passed the reviewing stand where sat the Führer along with European royalty, each team was expected to offer host, Adolph Hitler, the Nazi stiff-arm salute. Nation after nation passed the reviewing stand doing just that. Leading the procession, the Austrians gave the Nazi salute as they passed followed by the French who thrilled the Führer by giving the Nazi salute and holding it for an extended period. The Bulgarians outdid everyone by goose-stepping past as they saluted. But when the Americans passed the stand, they gave only the military-style *eyes right*.

Additionally, in the opening ceremony, flag bearers from every nation were expected to dip their country's flag while passing the reviewing stand, and each did so. But when time came for the Americans to pass the reviewing stand, they further upset the audience by adhering to the U.S. custom of dipping the American flag only to the President of the United States.

While nation after nation appeared awed by Germany's display of glitz and glamour, the Americans remained unimpressed. They were, after all, products of American beliefs held by independent American Minds.

Berlin to Beijing

While some things changed between the 1936 Berlin Olympics and the 2008 Beijing Olympics, others remained the same. One change was that Beijing's hosting cost more than the 1936 GDP of most attending nations. What remained the same was the attempt by godless nations to hide their godlessness beneath glitz and sparkle. Monumentally the same, singular American Minds competed in both competitions and shone in both competitions. Notable among them were Jesse Owens in 1936 and Michael Phelps in 2008.

Though much of Owens' Berlin adventure became exploited political myth, his four Olympic gold medals reveal valued aspects of beliefs held by his American Mind. Jesse was born in poverty. Because he was 'Negro,' Jesse could not live on campus while a student at Ohio State University. He and other black athletes and students had to find residence off campus. Worse, even though Jesse starred on the OSU track team, his race disqualified him from a scholarship; he worked nights in self-support. And still, he single-handedly raised himself above racial and economic trials to star in the 1936 Olympics.

Michael Phelps won eight gold swimming medals in Beijing. As a child, Michael was diagnosed with ADHD (Attention Deficit Hyperactive Disorder). Following older sisters who were swimmers and to release hyperactive energy, at his mother's urging seven-year-old Michael entered swimming. Because Michael entered swimming young and because he trained for hours each day for years on end, he developed acute coordination around the sport.

Chapter 6 * Belief's Consequences

When surgery for a broken wrist threatened training, rather than resting during healing, Michael kicked about the pool on a surfboard, racing teammates and building the leg muscles that no doubt produced the one-one-hundredth of a second victory over Serbia's Milorad Cavic in the hundred-meter butterfly. Underwater video shows that Cavic's legs had given out at the end and that Michael's leg-strength remained for that last great push.

The Great Belief

Obvious to even a casual observer, Jesse and Michael were driven beyond where the average person goes, giving rise to such questions as: What were the beliefs that drove them there? How were the beliefs that drove them different from those that drive the average person? And, where did those beliefs come from?

Given all beliefs that guide every human life from birth to death, the particularly American belief that drives minds like Jesse's and Michael's stands alone and apart in a vital category: *The American Mind believes it can.* As we shall see, this belief stems from America's earliest social attitude, emerging at the moment of America's founding.

Most minds around the world do not believe they can. Some wish they could, but the American Mind fully believes it can. It *expects* to. It demands this possibility and opposes any person or condition standing in its way. As happened with the Puritan colonizer, because his home country's social construct limited upward mobility, he came to the New World and built a country without that limitation. Like minds immigrate to America today, further seeding the American population with this genetic asset: *"I can, and I will rise! I must!"*

Perpetuated by this intense gene, this mind has compounded in natural selection, not happenstance, as one who asks life for more seeks out, marries, and reproduces with another doing the same thing. In the context of world history, the American Mind is an exceptional occurrence evidenced by America's fierce societal advance.

And the word *fierce* aptly describes how America happened. One need only observe fiercely bloodied Civil War battlefields; fiercely bloodied Native American battlefields; a decade of Depression-era financial strife inspired by fiercely over-optimistic financial speculation; and America offering its blood and treasure in other nations' fierce wars.

The American Mind is harsh yet refined; hard yet kind; exact yet forgiving. It is immutable. It is unstoppable. It is intelligent. It is intelligence. It is the greatest possession. It is *The Answer.*

Albert Einstein: *"The American lives even more for his goals, for the future, than the European. Life for him is always becoming, never being."*

Vince Lombardi and American Belief

Legendary football coach, Vince Lombardi stated, *"Winning isn't everything, but it's the only thing."* As a result, he received a great deal of criticism. When a displeased interviewer asked him if winning was Lombardi's *'be-all-end-all,'* this was his response: *"Winning? Well, I think it's only natural that anyone would think that to win is important. If you have any kind of dedication or any kind of backbone or spunk to you, you should try to be the best in your own profession regardless of what it is.*

"Anybody who has the idea that just to play or just to take part, and that's all that's necessary—I think he's in the wrong business. I think he's in the wrong country.

"I think one of the things that makes America great is: They try to be the best in everything they do. This, again, is signified by winning."

What did Coach Lombardi mean when he said, *"I think he's in the wrong country."* He didn't mean that all non-winners should leave the United States. He meant that the American citizen that doesn't take advantage of America's culture of freedom and opportunity is missing out on the chance to maximize personal progress. This was Lombardi's belief about being an American, about possessing an American way of thinking. Vince's life epitomized the American Mind.

Misunderstood and Underestimated

Many outside America's borders struggle to understand a mind that believes, as Einstein stated, in *'always becoming.'* That foreigner might both admire and condemn the American Mind and do so in the same breath. Self-confidence is condemned as arrogance. But self-confidence is not arrogance, although it may come across as such; if you can do it, it isn't bragging.

But how did the American Mind get like this? How did it become sufficiently brazen to make this demand upon life? Who gave it permission? Permission came from God, actually.

Today's American Mind, the mind that's attracted millions of immigrants, the mind that daily alters world history, is the natural consequence of a religious philosophy—belief—adopted centuries earlier by America's forbearers. Specifically, the revolutionary view that America's founders held about the Nature of Man led the American Mind to this place.[38]

The American Mind believes that God—not royalty, not a Führer, and certainly not any form of government—grants freedom. Great personal independence results from this belief in the divine source of rights. This independence combines with a specific and historically unique formula for daily decision-making to give an incomparable edge to possessors of the American Mind.

The founders did not adopt their belief in Divine Right by witnessing a great cosmic happening evidencing God. Rather, they adopted a moral technology unmatched in simplicity and in power by any

---

38. Quotation, author unknown: *"Until a man knows God, he cannot know himself."*

known comparison. Their new republic, and its resultant American Mind, happened because of three humble Judeo-Christian concepts: *1) moral agency—choosing the right; 2) repentance/forgiveness—leaving yesterday behind and proceeding upward and onward toward a better tomorrow; and 3) going and doing—an anxiously engaged work ethic.*

While not discussed by the founders as they will be here, these underpinnings of the American Mind have flowed consistently and powerfully beneath the surface of daily American life since early colonization. Misunderstood, mischaracterized, and subject to all manner of attack from without and within, these timeless principles accelerate mental prowess just as reliably today as at any time, and do so with incomparable results.

Answer to the Basic Question

The late and beloved American humorist, Art Buchwald, speculated as he removed himself from life-saving dialysis: *"I have no idea where I'm going, but here's the real question: What am I doing here in the first place?"* Employing inimitable and courageous humor, Art identified the inescapable conundrum that clerics, philosophers, scientists, and curious individuals have pondered since mankind first awakened to conscious thought.

When the American Mind answers the timeless query, *"What am I doing here?"* the answer descends from a singular belief in man's origin and purpose, a belief that began in the Middle East, and then fomented in Europe and England for some time prior to making its way across the Atlantic.

Adopted by America's Founding Fathers, this immigrating belief, while becoming the basis of American law, came also to form the basis of daily decision-making. And decision, we know, results in effort, and effort can be reaped in happiness and fulfillment on one hand and disappointment and tragedy on the other. So, what are the beliefs that determine which outcome will happen?

Belief's Two Routes

As belief moves through society and through individual minds toward acceptance and implementation, it follows one of two routes: Belief can be haphazardly encountered, randomly ingested, and partially followed. Or, belief can be purposefully analyzed and taught, and then accepted and followed.

Examining the ancient civilizations of Egypt, India, China, and Mesopotamia, Greece, and Rome, the beliefs that those societies came to accept about themselves and about the world around them varied greatly in specifics, but all shared a common thread. They all had a common denominator.

When this common denominator of belief is spread across the beliefs of the Aztec, Inca, Jew, Muslim, Buddhist, Hindu, and Christian, what do we find? The common denominator, the unifying feature of belief within these civilizations is the need that people feel, and have always felt, to make sense of life. Natural curiosity drives mankind to seek this answer—*The Answer*—to come to an understanding of human existence such that life can be dealt with effectively and happily.

To beings capable of loving and hating; of hurting and healing; of laughing and weeping; of dejection and joyful celebration; of saving life and taking life; of bravery and cowardice; of self-discipline and licentiousness; of virtue and vice; of good and evil, fitting these behavioral opposites into an understandable paradigm becomes essential to any progress that a mind—and the society in which that mind dwells—hopes to make. What is life without this finding or without searching for this finding?

The Search for Belief

A mind might approach this quest for meaning by observing the world at large and try to make its physics understandable as did Aristotle, Pythagoras, Ptolemy, Copernicus, Galileo, da Vinci, Kepler, Newton, and Einstein. Or a mind might seek life's essence through Muhammad, Buddha, Confucius, Moses, or Jesus and try to make birth, death, and the human conscience make sense. But upon scanning the human experience physically or spiritually, the immediate discovery is that differences in belief exist—even vast differences among the individuals just mentioned.

A mind searching for absolutes in belief faces the impossible: Once belief becomes absolute, it is called knowledge or fact. Belief is assumption, not knowledge or fact, and, as no two minds make identical assumptions about anything, the same belief reduces to varieties of actions across its adherents.

While people respond differently to the same belief, the cumulative outcome of a country's belief source becomes measurable in many societal categories. Consider that cultural products such as law and public policy, standard of living, social and vocational opportunities including upward social mobility, educational opportunity, and public health, express the results of a society's deepest beliefs, especially its religious beliefs.

In the Middle East, China, India, Africa, Europe, North and South America, and in all places about the globe where hope and expectation exist for young people, those who love and guide them face the same challenge, and it's a formidable one: Knowing that character succeeds regardless of all else, youth leaders, church leaders, schoolteachers, and parents and grandparents hope to instill beliefs that inspire the highest character. But which beliefs do so, where are they found, and what substantiates their value?

Looking Back

History records countless consequences sponsored by countless beliefs. From these consequences, the outcome of one culture may be compared to that of another as though a particular culture represents a single human life. America's beliefs have maximized the lives of millions upon millions of her people. With reason, America's early European-derived beliefs were not pure, and the nation's fierce history reflects such; few conquests leave no objectors. But in spite of her difficult past, America's classical beliefs have advanced her people with historically blinding speed. They did so, and do so, not only for those choosing to be guided by them but also for those supported by the accomplishments of the observers.

Throughout her short history, America has known aberrations in these original beliefs. In sorrow, she suffered a bitter civil war where 600,000 lives were lost defending opposite extremes of what started out as the same principles arising from the same beliefs.

Though both sides were present in old Philadelphia when the belief of 1776 became the foundation for American law in 1787, the beliefs of the North and of the South were not the same when sufficient pressure came to bear, and the nation exploded in appalling violence.

The failure of the South to fully embrace belief in the divine origin of man—and so of the God-granted rights of all men—in 1776, resulted in a cultural gulf so vile that it demanded, at last, to be filled with pain, suffering, blood, and death.

The decimation of American natives by colonizing Europeans resulted from original belief's collision with expediency. While these colliding cultures endured outrageous violence mutually administered, the side with the most advanced civil structure, and the most guns, won.

In addition to America's Civil and Native American Wars, America has seen periods like the Sixties when drug use and sexual license washed over a portion of her young people, leaving philosophical residue that today forms the American Left.[39] But America has survived it all, greatly prospered, and has done so for the persistence of three humble beliefs: *moral agency, repentance/forgiveness, and going and doing*. By design, it is the humility of these beliefs that generates their potency, for, from small and simple things are great things brought to pass.[40]

Origins of Belief

Not all of man's beliefs come by the same path, and particular results may be ascribed to each divide in the anthropological roadway. The notable American author, John Steinbeck, was close friends with a marine biologist named Ed Ricketts. Out of sheer friendship, Steinbeck would accompany Ricketts on specimen-gathering expeditions into the many estuaries that line Mexico's Sea of Cortez.

In trading with the natives who helped them there, they discovered that though an object like a boat or harpoon could have a price, other commodities like time, heat, cold, health, or beauty could not, and no amount of explaining could convince the natives otherwise; they would not accept money or trinkets for time spent helping the Americans. This was something they apparently loved to do, obviously feeling compensated in other ways.

In contrast, the American buys and sells heat, cold, clean air, time

---

[39]. The sixties counterculture: A small segment of university-attending baby boomers rebelled against American society's historical norms. Abandoning Judeo-Christianity's self-discipline, they embraced pleasure, especially sexual and drug-induced escapism. Seeking to justify their licentiousness, they opposed their parent's religion, they opposed democracy, and they opposed America. Embracing the social philosophies of anarchistic theorists Karl Marx and Chairman Mao, these same people lead today's American Left and today's Democrat Party. This philosophy thrives in academia today as well, carried there by this same group where they fill vulnerable young minds with ideas proven to yield only misery, lost hope, and failure: Socialism and Communism.

[40]. Scripture: *"Now ye may suppose that this is foolishness in me; but behold I say unto you, that by small and simple things are great things brought to pass; and small means in many instances doth confound the wise."*

certainly, and health and beauty. Contrary to the simplicity observed in Mexico, the American may become burdened and spent just trying to earn enough to pay for all that free enterprise convinces him that he needs.

If permitted to remain ignorant of the complications facing the Mexican native, the American might long for such simplicity. The native, on the other hand, subject to constant heat and cold, to the misery of malnutrition, to infection and disease, and to endless toil just for daily sustenance, may well envy Yankee luxury.

While this example contrasts differences in the cultural beliefs of nations, one need not leave America's shores to find belief differences between individuals just as great. But of the beliefs that cause differences between individuals, which belief, or belief system, causes the greatest difference?

Could it be that the belief system that drives *personal progress* most effectively is what causes the greatest difference? And if this is so, what is the belief system that drives personal progress best? Can it be identified? What is its origin?

What about belief systems like Socialism and Communism that discourage personal progress? Where should they rank among societal prescriptions for personal progress?

Benjamin Franklin and the Power of Belief

The belief essentials that produce the rarity of the American Mind predated America's Revolutionary War by multiple millennia, coalescing into something socially identifiable a few decades prior to, during, and a few decades after that conflict. These socially identifiable traits are witnessed conspicuously in the mind of early patriot, Benjamin Franklin.

In fact, a startling parallel exists between Franklin's life and what the American Mind has come to be. From an examination of Franklin's life comes the query already noted that has answered itself in millions of American lives since. Franklin: *"How does one live a life that is useful, virtuous, worthy, moral, and spiritually meaningful?"*

In a life that answered this question for all the world to see—and Franklin did not live the life of a saint—he rose from familial ostracism, a second-grade education, and moral wandering to world-renown heights in science, politics, philosophy, philanthropy, personal wealth, and peer respect. Franklin demonstrated what happens when a person with a devoted work ethic and guided by a moral framework finds himself within a society of unprecedented freedom. How many millions have followed him using that same formula?

Chapter 7
Freedom, Independence, and Personal Progress

*F*oremost among America's many qualities has always been opportunity—opportunity for any citizen so motivated to design a path through life, and then follow that path through to an improved circumstance. Until recently, such personal advancement was possible in America because America's governmental policy strove to maximize each citizen's *freedom to choose*.

It was nothing more than the American Mind's desire for individual independence and freedom that drove it to revolt against King George in the first place. It was the American Mind's independent bent that went on to build a great and independent society staffed with great and independent minds. And it is that same independent streak that assures America's future. America's current governing policy will not. America's current politicians certainly will not.

Why? Because a populace with an independent attitude threatens the State's politicians and employees. It always has. In Stalin's statist Russia and Mao's statist China, the State and its political leadership removed anyone expressing an independent mind. Such parties were and continue to be removed, disappeared, murdered. Tens of millions have thus perished in Russia and in China.

Maintaining sufficient freedom for each individual to independently maximize upward mobility is a difficult challenge for any government to face. The U.S. government's lead politicians have lately begun a vigorous campaign against the independent American Mind.[41] Why? Because providing sufficient freedom for an individual's unrestricted upward mobility leaves government with limited power. Government does not like its power to be limited. As government is a business unto itself, such limitation threatens government as it loses the ability to dictate its own scope, size, and especially how its operatives are remunerated.

And government isn't the only force that mounts against the independent mind; anyone attempting the independent American Mind can plan on criticism from many quarters in its moment of embarkation. Staking out a clear course for one's life and sticking to it threatens those unwilling to accept the same challenge. No one appreciates looking inadequate by comparison. Thus, neutralizing the comparison becomes the tactic of choice. Think of the recent destruction of persons daring to mention individual responsibility and accountability. Dare one mention 47%?[42]

At the time of America's founding, contributors to the process made clear that they could not and would not suffer aristocratic—elitist—governmental or religious rule, social castes, or any threat to the American Mind's independent qualities. In terms of political construct, they would only tolerate a government with limited scope,

---

41. Note the shrillness of Democrat's incessant harping about *'White supremacy'* and 'White privilege' when they are the ones demanding to be supreme. How about misleading with vaccines that aren't vaccines, masks that demonstrably don't prevent, utterly ineffective social distancing, and more, and shouting down or cancelling discordance. The list is endless, and for what? Power, money, and celebrity.

42. Mitt Romney 2012 presidential campaign: *"47% of Americans receive some sort of government support."* True, but Romney was condemned for bringing it up. Having dependents gives government a reason for being. Why do virtually all government employees belong to the political party that once enslaved, and that now continues to enslave?

Chapter 7 * Freedom, Independence, and Personal Progress

especially when compared to any other form of government known at the time. Recall the story behind the Bill of Rights:

Led principally by the American Mind of Virginian—though British-born—Patrick Henry, a need was seen for even more protection for the individual from governmental imposition than what the Constitution promised. Henry and fellow colonials' recent subjugation to British governmental tyranny had left so foul a taste that, upon reflection, they could not bring themselves to trust even the government they had just created. They demanded, and the Bill of Rights promised, even greater protection—from government—of their hard-won civil liberties.

Re-reading Patrick Henry's cry for freedom refreshes the memory of just how acute the concept of liberty had become at the time of America's founding. Henry: *"Is life so dear, or peace so sweet, as to be purchased at the price of chains and slavery? Forbid it, Almighty God! I know not what course others may take; but as for me, give me liberty or give me death!"*

Taste the passion of Henry's pleading! This demand for individual liberty and independence frightens those among the American citizenry who do not possess an American Mind.[43] Academic elites characterize this independent streak as uncivilized, crude, selfish, and uneducated. They cannot understand it: *"Can't we all just share what you produce?"*

To say that those not possessing an American Mind cannot understand its fierce demand for freedom and independence is an understatement. Entire societies cannot understand the American Mind's independent bent either. Why? This disconnect happens because they cannot grasp the American Mind's belief regarding the Nature of Man.

And it is this belief regarding the Nature of Man—a belief born

---

43. President Andrew Jackson called the American Mind's independent nature *stubborn virtue*.

of Judeo-Christian influence—that distinguishes the American Mind, a mind that in the surplus of freedom granted by its Constitution and guaranteed by its Bill of Rights has raised the possibilities of humankind in a shorter span and with greater influence than mankind ever knew previously.

For the individual to continue benefitting from this unusual view, and harvesting its rewards, the beliefs that propagate it must be passed from one generation to the next. These vital teachings were greatly neutralized in the elections of 1992, 1996, 2008, and 2012 and in 2020 placed in absolute jeopardy. For America, and for you and your family to maximize life's potential, these principles must be defended. But how can that be done amidst governmental obstruction, greedy and mediocre politicians, a subjective rather than objective media, and societal godlessness?

Examples of Dependent Minds

Glaring for every American to see are examples of *dependent* minds: Native Americans herded onto reservations and African-Americans caged in either public housing or within *white supremacy and white privilege* propaganda are perfect examples. As Henry Ford put it: *"Any man who thinks he can be happy and prosperous by letting the government take care of him better take a closer look at the American Indian."* Ford was not demeaning the Native American; rather, he was making clear how removing a person's survival initiative destroys that person's self-respect and feeling of self-worth.

Yes, Native Americans did lose the war against invading Europeans, and conquerors do dictate terms. With the passing of time, much has been done to make amends for broken treaties and inhumane treatment. But allowing emotional resentment to linger is unwise and unproductive. The past is what it is. Today, the Native American, and everyone else that has been delt a difficult hand, must make the best of whatever that hand is. One's life outcome is not bound to one's beginning. One's life begins where one is, not where one should have been, or could have been, or might have been. Overcoming life's obstacles rather than submitting to them is how to advance one's life.

A mind whose every physical need is met by someone else, who never faces each day with the need to survive by its own efforts, languishes in stagnation at best and suffers damage at worst. Such a mind serves as little more than a sensor, measuring its surroundings for threats to survival, becoming loveless and animalistic in nature. Where is self-respect in this scenario? Where is personal progress in this scenario?

Consider that over 70% of African American children are born to single mothers. How are these little ones expected to compete with children born to wedded, supportive parents? Numbers tell the tale: 90% of prison inmates come from fatherless homes, and 71% of felons are born to single women. Because these numbers have worsened over recent decades with nothing done to reverse the trend, might politicians be using the system to political advantage? Is *'welfare'* not slavery by another name?

In the Civil War, Democrats were willing to destroy the nation to keep their slaves. They do the same thing today. It is no stretch to state that while Stalin and Mao murdered tens of millions of their own, what Democrats are doing to African-Americans today is no better. Incalculable is the number of African-American lives neutralized by political policy that rewards destructive behavior. Would it not be better to reward good behavior, behavior that advances human life?

Remember that for at least a century prior to 1619 and for two centuries thereafter, the African continent's principal export was slaves, men and women captured and sold by fellow Africans. In 1807, when the United Kingdom declared an end to the slave trade, those objecting most strenuously were African kings. This ugly fact never makes it into the story. Descendants of African slave traders practice the same thing today on their own racial brothers and sisters, caging them within governmental dependency or bogus threats of *white privilege* and *white supremacy*—leaving them there to rot until it's time to harvest their votes.[44]

Self-Reliance

A mind that depends upon itself takes pride in good scholastic and moral performance, in building a career, supporting a family, and preparing for aging. Such a mind finds satisfaction and meaning in *going and doing*. Such a mind is unhappy waiting for life to happen and instead makes it happen. Such a mind proves unmatched when life's inevitable challenges may and do crash down.[45] Making the first selection—independently building oneself—makes future encounters with adversity significantly less threatening and calamitous.

The mind that nourishes itself with continuous spiritual and intellectual care enjoys incomparable advantage in the world. Such a mind embraces life's panorama with ever-increasing ability and from ever-higher plateaus of understanding. Such a mind stands apart. Such a mind produces independently-derived and often unique solutions to life's difficulties. Such a mind welcomes the risk of career and other competitions because with competition comes winning, and winning makes things better. Such a mind respects God, family, and country. Such a mind respects itself. Such a mind basks in the glow of spouse, children, grandchildren, and great-grandchildren, all marching triumphantly into the future as a family.

---

44. The Obama administration thrilled to have added 14 million souls to the food stamp program. Remember who it was that sold their own people into slavery for hundreds of years.

45. Abraham Lincoln: *"The best way to predict the future is to create it."*

Section 4
Religion and the American Mind

A major determinant in the life of every individual who has ever lived is what today is called that individual's *worldview*. One's worldview arises from what one has been taught and from what one has experienced. At the core of one's worldview stands religion, and everyone has a religion whether one thinks so or not, whether God figures in or not.

In examining the effect that various religious views have upon the mind, this work will delve most deeply into Judeo-Christianity's effect. An examination of America's founding documents demonstrates just how weighty Judeo-Christianity's doctrine and Judeo-Christianity's God were. But this is not where our journey begins.

To grasp the extent of religion's influence in forming the American Mind and the intellect within it, we must track each period of change in western civilization's religious thinking, starting with the earliest written records.

Our trek begins over four-thousand years ago with a Hebrew prophet named Abraham, the first architect, one could say, of what the American Mind would become. We will then progress to Moses, on to Jesus, and then to Constantine and his Nicene Conference. Next follows an examination of the Reformation and its aftermath, finally arriving at the American Restoration.

Following this historical thread, we will see how Judeo-Christianity as an evolving intellectual technology came, bit-by-bit, to lift the individual life to an ever-improving circumstance.

Also evident within this review is the technological progress of Western Man and how that progress phased slightly behind Western Man's moral advance. The average historian would reverse this process and say that science, or the scientific method, came first, and that is what spurred mankind's societal advance. But that's not how it happened nor how it continues to play out.

Spiritual enlightenment precedes social and scientific enlightenment, whether on an individual or worldwide basis. It must, for a darkened mind cannot, does not, never has, and never will produce light.

In evidence of this claim, refer to those scientific achievers listed on page 64 of this book. Even a modest examination of each life reveals two key commonalities: 1) Divine acknowledgment, even piety, and 2) Unquenchable curiosity, the foremost trait of an enlightened mind.

Basking in this same divine enlightenment, though more refined in the interim since Abraham began the process, America's founders formulated the most liberal legal basis for government the world had yet seen or that it has seen since—one that the American Left cannot afford to leave in place. The trust that America's founders placed in the individual citizen's conduct sprang from their assumption that Judeo-Christian ethics would guide their countrymen's behavior, and until recently it did.

In formulating a revolutionary society, America's pioneer politicians combined their personal views of governmental structure with

Chapter 7 * Freedom, Independence, and Personal Progress

those of Europeans Locke and Rousseau[46] and came up with an entirely new form of government; one that the world could scarcely believe was taking shape; one that the foreign observer was certain would fail; and one that the American Left is openly warring against today. What person would be simple enough to believe that a people, especially a country of common people, could self-govern? *"Don't these fools understand that they need a monarch, or at least an elite ruling class to manage their affairs?"*

Well, Americans did successfully govern themselves and will continue doing so as long as America's founding principles remain active. Even a casual examination shows how, after piloting America for over 240 years, the same Judeo-Christian encouragements—intellectual techniques, actually—became genetically embedded within portions of the American population.

But first let us return to exploring how this intellectual technology came into being in the first place and with force sufficient that it has not only survived intact but has prospered in a land where law specifically bans governmental meddling in matters of individual conscience, something it now insists upon doing.[47] [48]

We will also see how, today, this vital intellectual component is on trial for its life, attacked by a Leftist ideology far more hazardous to

---

46. England's Locke was a priest before becoming a social philosopher and writer. France's Rousseau lived his teenage years with Jesuit priests, and his resultant social thinking heavily reflected that influence. Both men, nearly one-hundred years apart, recognized man as God's creation, not government's, and believed that public policy should reflect the fact.

47. First Amendment: *"Congress shall make no law respecting an establishment of religion, or prohibiting the free exercise thereof . . ."* but, if a person fails to grant a marriage license to a homosexual couple believing that homosexuality is a sin, or if a person fails to support abortion due to their *free exercise* of religion, they may be fired, bankrupted, fined, jailed, ridiculed in public, and left to stand without libel protection.

48. According to the American Left: Christianity is nothing more than masked intolerance and hypocrisy. According to them, the phrases *civil liberty* and *religious liberty* are code for intolerance, racism, sexism, homophobia, Islamophobia, and discrimination. Questions: What motivates the American Left to demean personal conviction, religious or otherwise? Do commandments handed down by God stand for nothing? Will the person with sufficient authority to overturn God's statutes please step forward!

personal freedom and individual progress than what British overreach prior to 1776 ever was. It must be pointed out that the most valued asset that a human being can possess is an independent mind and sufficient governmental room—freedom—in which that mind can operate. No issue threatens Leftist ideology more than a mind that demands enough freedom in which to maximize personal progress. In many societies, such minds are still removed today. Russia, China, some Middle Eastern and some South American countries, to name a few, continue to remove dissenters. In America, such minds can depend upon continued oppression from the Left,[49] cancellation being the most common method. But life has always been thus—good against evil—and for this reason, fortifying one's life against such opposition ranks among life's most important safeguards.

---

49. The arrogance and elitism of the American Left astounds. Compounding the issue is the Left forcing obedience to Leftist ideals. If Leftist ideology is so remarkable, why must it be forcefully imposed? Obamacare, anyone?

Chapter 8
Religion 101

Religion is at once a dear topic and an angry topic, full of hot buttons that get people riled up. People kill in the name of religion. People die in the name of religion. A nation's foundational institutions like its law and public policy, its culture or cultures, its educational structure and slant, and its economic fortunes all spring from its composite beliefs regarding the Nature of Man.

On a personal level, every person holds notions about the origin of the human conscience, about man's essence, man's soul, and man's destiny. These notions usually come through an organized system of instruction but may also be picked up in places like freshman dormitories.

Religion's Smaller Parts

Tackling this enormous subject is simplified by breaking it down into smaller parts. Picture a sheet of paper divided into two columns. The column on the left lists the beliefs of the believer. The column on the right lists the belief's source. The belief's source may be an organized religion like Catholicism or Islam or an unorganized religion like the one that took hold in Nazi Germany.

The belief column is categorized into a soul's three phases of development and passage, if such a thing as a soul exists at all. Phase I explains the possibility of a soul's pre-earthly beginning and any experience it may have had prior to showing up in the maternity ward. Phase II explains the goal of, or reason for, a soul's earthly passage. Phase III explains the possibility, structure, and objective of a soul's post-earthly life.

God in Religion

God sometimes figures within these column notations, and sometimes not. Sometimes the right hand, or source notation, carries the name of an organized denomination. Sometimes a source has no denominational name at all but must be noted as a spring of religious belief, still, because it answers religion's three classical phases.

Also, the two columns do not always match up because the beliefs of many people do not coincide with those of their professed denomination or source. Is a Catholic who fails to stand against killing the unborn really a Catholic?

Everyone has a Religion

Everyone capable of responding to the soul's three phases—pre-earthly life, earthly life, and after-life—espouses a religion. For example, a person who holds that life begins as the baby's body exits the womb; that following birth life is survived day-to-day by learned skills; and that death simply ends it all, has the most basic of religions. Godless and uncomplicated, it qualifies as that person's religion, still, because it covers its proponent's belief about religion's three classical phases. Darwinists fill this religion. Atheists fit here, too.

A contrasting God-based view may give great detail to the human spirit's origin, detailing grand experiences it may have had prior to showing up as an embodied human being. This belief may insist that every earthly thought and deed exert a ranking influence in an inevitable judgment, and that earthly passage holds the ever-present opportunity for a personal relationship with the Almighty.

Finally, this view may suggest that the human spirit is eternal in nature and will continue acquiring intellectual and charitable perfection forever beyond the grave, even to the point of gaining knowledge to the level of God's understanding.

This is a complicated religion inclusive of God and of an ultimate, infinite, and yet definable destiny for the soul. While referred to by the denominational name under which it was organized, it belongs to each believer in an intimate sense, uniquely forming that person as that person adapts life to that denomination's particular beliefs the way that person does.

Another person, having received identical instruction must, owing to the difference in each individual's intellectual background and diligence in adapting behavior to creed, form religious views and that person's resultant life-outcome differently.

This brings up two amusing but pivotally important points: Firstly, no two people enjoy the same religion. And secondly, regardless of what one's religion may be, simple or complicated, known by its denominational name or not named at all, each individual's religion, by all feats of logic, is measured by one God who, to be just, promotes one criterion.

This is assuming that God exists at all. If God does not exist, then each tenant of each denomination has simply been invented—made up—the same process those not professing God employ in coming up with their religion.

God and Justice

To be just, as God is reported to be, His criteria must spread across varying cultures, fitting each cultural sphere within a domain of good and evil such that progress against evil is measurable between the Almighty and each of His children.[50] [51] This is assuming once more that the Almighty really exists; and that human beings are His spirit children.

This is the dogma side of religion, the righthand column in this analysis. It consists of various sets of explanations and rules put forward by each organized denomination and by each unorganized group of theorists. Adherence to these rules, or commandments, or standards, or tenants, as they are called, is each group's method of advancing the believer's character toward a state-of-being that that creed sees as the soul's ultimate fulfillment.

Some creeds promise this fulfillment far beyond earth's horizon: Islam. Others get to it more quickly, some right on the spot: born-again evangelicals. Others see no need getting to it at all: Darwinists and Atheists.

Getting to it is the reason God-based denominations issue behavioral standards in the first place. *Getting to it* is the process of building one's character and charitability. Since God-based religions believe that it is strength of character and purity of heart that advance one's life, this process cannot be too soon begun. And this leads to another discovery in explaining the American Mind:

A person's spiritual, intellectual, and material prosperity can and will be no greater than the opportunities that person's religion offers. Recall that America's founders based their reasoned approach to government upon socio-Christian ideals expounded by Locke and Rousseau, compounded with the ponderous influence of their own Judeo-Christian logic and Judeo-Christian backgrounds.

---

50. Scripture: *"For behold, the Lord doth grant unto all nations, of their own nation and tongue, to teach his word, yea, in wisdom, all that he seeth fit that they should have; therefore, we see that the Lord doth counsel in wisdom, according to that which is just and true."*

51. Scripture: *"And even unto the great and last day, when all people, and all kindreds, and all nations and tongues shall stand before God, to be judged of their works, whether they be good or whether they be evil."*

Think once again of Adam Smith's theory of *rational self-interest*: While Smith connected moral discipline only to advancing a nation's economic prospects,[52] the extended result of moral sophistication upon a citizenry is significantly broader. Stated plainly, the more sophistication with which a person employs a sense of moral obligation—Smith's rationality—the more refined that person's behavior becomes, and consequently, the greater the potential outcome for that person's life, not to mention the lives of that person's family, peers, and nation.[53]

God-Based versus Godless in Shaping One's Worldview

The view one holds of the Nature of Man—God-based or not—more firmly anchors a person's worldview than anything else. These examples make the point:

In the first instance, picture a youth kneeling alone in a quiet grove of trees, sent there by a conscientious parent, clergyman, or by the youth's own initiative, that prompted the youth to seek God through direct pleading. Imagine the youth's assumption of being the child of a loving Heavenly Father to whom he is presenting a certain problem. Imagine the youth accepting that earth exists as a campus of trial and that personal growth and joy come from conquering such trial. Imagine the youth's feeling of self-worth from believing that someone higher than himself loves him, cares about how things turn out, and stands ready to assist. Imagine the sense of purpose in having God as his partner in mastering life's difficulties. Other people fit into this person's life as traveling companions, all striving to arrive at a good place. Evil and trial, even suffering, make sense because they necessarily form the opposition that must be overcome to develop this

---

52. Again: Protestant Christian nations are 40% more productive than non-Protestant nations. Why?

53. Think, here, of people of renown whose base acts become exampled among young people. What influence would righteousness have had instead?

young person's charitable and moral character.

Now consider another youth standing in the same grove, sent there to observe Darwin's natural selection. The youngster witnesses a coyote catch, kill, and devour, a baby rabbit. Viewing life as a strictly organic experience, nature has now confirmed it to be so. Only the youth himself, and perhaps his family, really care how things turn out. There is no Heavenly Parent to care. This person views others rather as competitors than companions; a world of coyotes and bunnies. Rather than seeing trial as an opportunity to strengthen, trial threatens and frightens, creating uncertainty rather than self-confidence. This point of view casts fellow beings either as inferior and unworthy or as superior and threatening, resulting in a lonely and prejudicial worldview.

There is a third case: Much of life has passed for this person. This person doesn't bother to meditate or to observe. This person dares not reassess life. Triumph has been accredited to skill and misfortune to bad luck. God lingers as an ethereal concept molded to answer circumstance after the fact. Where is personal progress in this view?

The Religious Cycle

Because life's trials come and go, one's spiritual dedication rarely remains constant. In this cycling of spiritual diligence, prosperity has a way of diminishing dependence upon God. Vain pride surges during times of ease and prosperity. Looking in the mirror, it's easy to identify genius in the face looking back at you.

The opposite of prosperity, hardship begets humility, and the humbled person becomes teachable. How could the face in the mirror have been so stupid? Along with making a person teachable, humility aligns with modesty and meekness, and meekness is not weakness[54].

Consider the generation that conquered the Great Depression;

---

54. Definition of meek: Enduring injury with patience and without resentment; submissive in spirit; not violent.

that defeated Nazism; that challenged Soviet Communism, ultimately tearing down the Berlin Wall; and, from there, fostered and cheered the freeing of countless families by the Soviet Union's dismantling. Compare those magnificent men and women to some of their children, the pampered flower children of the counter-culture Sixties—young people so brilliant that they countered their parent's culture with one they invented: *"Place a flower in your hair and make love not war."* Hedonism anyone?

God and Logic

Defining God however one might, should God exist logic demands that God must be the ultimate fact. Understanding that fact speeds personal development as one adapts behavior to this critical knowledge. Einstein again: *"I want to know God's thoughts. The rest are details."*[55] Albert's statement implies that—should God exist—a person that does not acknowledge God does not and cannot understand himself.

For those whose religion includes the God of Abraham, Moses, and Jesus, the God whom America's founders referenced in establishing the American republic, gathering perspective about the interaction these early prophets had with God becomes first in our historical review. Reviewing the thoughts and activities of Abraham, Moses, and Jesus reveals how Western Man's behavioral refinement progressed—how the American Mind got here from there.

---

55. Albert Einstein: *"Science without religion is lame; religion without science is blind."*

Chapter 9
Ancient Architects – Abraham to Constantine

Over 4,000 years ago, a righteous man named Abraham—Father Abraham as he is warmly and accurately referred to—began an intellectual revolution in the Middle East of enormous earthly consequence, certainly in terms of Western Civilization.

Accepting Adam's time as the formative period for the human conscience, by Abraham's time some centuries later numerous splinter groups had broken away from traditions that earlier had supported at least reasonable civility. These groups saw the world in as many lights as there were groups—tribes—and many among them were not nice people. They did a lot of bad things, things that don't help much when one would like to lead a productive, peaceful, and fulfilling life, and to have one's children do so as well.

According to the account, key to Abraham's bringing order to civil chaos was his receipt of authorization from God. Abraham's attempt was initiated by God, was supervised by God, and was meant to serve God's purposes. After all, the individuals to benefit from heavenly covenants and peaceful social order were God's children. Abraham considered them his children too, and many were his descendants as generations passed.

As with Adam, Noah, and Enoch before him, God authorized Abraham to undertake the project by conferring a *priesthood* upon him. Called by God to serve under *priesthood authority*, Abraham became the authorized vessel through whom God could and did communicate his will. Were the attempt not authorized by God—had it not been under priesthood direction and authority—it would simply have been a good man attempting a good thing and little would likely be known of it today.

Most notably, God formed with Abraham a bond, a religious contract known as the Abrahamic Covenant.[56][57] It was under this celestial collaboration that the West's earliest statutes came to be—statutes aimed at elevating mankind's behavior.

Circumcision of all males at eight days of age became the sign of the covenant. The body of the covenant—the obligation of each party within the covenant—became the following: For God's part, he promised to bless Abraham's seed that they would number with the sands of the sea and fill the earth, forming mighty nations, and they have.

(Incidentally, the name *Abraham* means *father of multitudes*. Abraham went from being called Abram—*exalted father*—to being called Abraham—*father of multitudes*. Along the way in his relationship with God and fellowmen, Abraham impressed God sufficiently that he was selected to undertake this special mission, not unlike what happens in all lives—according to Judeo-Christian premise—when answered by Heaven with the means to an end. But in today's world, name changes don't necessarily accompany spiritual changes, at least to the degree of Abram to Abraham.)

---

56. Scripture: KJV (King James Version), Old Testament, book of Genesis.
57. The prophet Abraham is a foundational figure in Jewish, Christian, and Islamic religious belief.

Obedience Precedes Blessings

This next point cannot be overlooked nor over-emphasized: Abraham first qualified as one upon whom God could depend before gaining God's support in his cause, not the other way around. It appears that this is how God works his will; faith precedes the miracle.[58] Obedience to God's commandments precedes and is integral to expressing one's faith,[59] thereby preparing the way for improved divine association.

Spiritual science happens within spiritual realms, and throughout the course of spiritual quests. Humility, righteousness, sincerity, charity, and obedience to God's commandments, qualify the hopeful petitioner. It makes sense that little demand can be made upon God until God's principles are understood and met.[60]

Hollywood explains that in a crunch one can plead with Heaven for a bailout. Remember that Heaven is not Hollywood. While God is not hard, he does appear to be exact. He appears to respect heavenly law above personalities. His processes appear to go both ways better *after* the human side submits to his will, not before. If this is so, and Judeo-Christian evidence suggests that it is, God remains committed but awaits human commitment prior to furthering the relationship. This does not preclude mercy on His behalf, something that all appreciate when bestowed. It does suggest that submissiveness and obedience to His commandments prior to pleading might not be misplaced.

Back to Abraham and the Abrahamic Covenant: God blessed

---

58. Scripture: *"For if there be no faith among the children of men God can do no miracle among them; wherefore, he showed not himself until after their faith."* Second Scripture: *"Behold I say unto you, Nay; for it is by faith that miracles are wrought; and it is by faith that angels appear and minister unto men; wherefore, if these things have ceased wo be unto the children of men, for it is because of unbelief, and all is vain."*

59. Scripture: *"For faith is the substance of things hoped for, the evidence of things unseen."* While faith has an element of substantive hope, it is more importantly evidence of the unseen and is verified by action accordingly prompted.

60. Scripture: *"I, the Lord, am bound when ye do what I say. When ye do not what I say, ye have no promise."*

Abraham that should his people *keep the way of the Lord* and *exercise justice and judgment* in dealing with their fellowmen that they would prosper and that by his seed *all nations of the Earth would be blessed in him.*[61]

God promised Abraham that the Messiah would come through his lineage, and Jesus Christ did. God promised Abraham certain lands as an inheritance for his posterity—the same Middle Eastern lands today disputed by Israelis, Palestinians, and other Arab factions. These lands are being quarreled over by the two principal branches of Abraham's seed: Hebrews—Israelis—descended from his promised son Isaac, born of his Hebrew wife Sarah; and Muslims, descended from his half-Hebrew son Ishmael, *born after the flesh* of the Egyptian woman Hagar.[62]

For Abraham's part of the covenant, he and his family needed to observe the *way of the Lord* in exercising *justice and judgment* and prosperity, and a homeland would be theirs. Not only would they prosper in their promised homeland if they obeyed God's pronouncements, but all nations of the earth would benefit from the civil and intellectual contributions of this *chosen people*, and all this has happened.

Abraham's Seed

But both Jews and Muslims have struggled since to keep their part of the bargain. Though the Muslim has prospered at times, fulfilling prophesy during the Ottoman period, Islam has not made the social, academic, scientific, or philanthropic contributions to mankind, expected from such promising prophecy.

---

61. Scripture *"For I know him, that he will command his children and his household after him, and they shall keep the way of the Lord, to do justice and judgment; that the Lord may bring upon Abraham that which he hath spoken of him."*

62. Scripture: *"Now Sarai, Abram's wife, bare him no children: and she had an handmaid, an Egyptian whose name was Hagar . . . And Sarai, Abram's wife took Hagar her maid the Egyptian, after Abram had dwelt ten years in the land of Canaan, and gave her to her husband Abram to be his wife . . . And Hagar bare Abram a son: and Abram called his son's name, which Hagar bare, Ishmael."*

Though never to the grand scope of his half-cousin's Ottoman era, the odd times when the Hebrew has lived *the way of the Lord*, he has prospered and occupied his promised homeland. But falling into periods of disobedience to moral statute and the inevitable loss of character that accompanies wobbly standards, he has faltered, suffered relentless persecution, and faced literal annihilation.

But in spite of his troubles, would the West be the same without Jewish influence? Is there doubt of God's promise that *all nations of the earth shall be blessed in the seed of Abraham?* What would life be like today without Jesus' influence upon the world, especially the western world, and especially the American world?[63]

In addition to Jesus, take a moment and list all those of Jewish heritage of whom you are aware that have contributed to mankind's advance. The list is long, varied, and simply remarkable. No genetic pool matches it. One must ask: *"How did this happen?"* One must also ask: *"Why has Islam not contributed similarly to mankind's forward march?"*

Going back to Abraham: Following Abraham's demise, life did not go well for the Hebrews. With the loss of Abraham's leadership, his followers abandoned the character-building moral code that his Abrahamic Covenant had wrought, and the Hebrews fell into captivity; they became enslaved to the Egyptians.

Then, along came Moses, finally.

Moses

History is vague in the interim between Abraham and Moses apart from the story of Joseph, Abraham's great-grandson, being delivered into Egyptian slavery by his brothers.

As in Abraham's time, in Moses' time Egypt maintained itself

---

63. John Adams, 2nd US president: *"The Hebrews have done more to civilize men than any other nation. If I were an atheist, and believed in blind eternal fate, I should still believe that fate had ordained the Jews to be the most essential instrument for civilizing the nations."*

the chief political and economic power in the region. Moses, with his unique birth circumstance—a Hebrew by blood raised as an Egyptian—found the Hebrews enslaved to the Egyptians. Discovering that he was Hebrew and not Egyptian caused Moses to rebel against his Egyptian friends, and he began fighting for Hebrew freedom.

Moses had his hands full in that rebellion, but he was not alone. Like Father Abraham, Moses formed an alliance with God. After living for years in strict obedience to God's pronouncements, Moses sought God's help in freeing his People, and God responded. He inspired Moses, empowering him with the same priesthood authority earlier bestowed upon Abraham. God then showered Moses with miracles—miracles sufficient to convince the Egyptians to let his people go, which they eventually and grudgingly did.[64]

But the freed Hebrew had known nothing but slavery. Wandering the desert in search of food was not his idea of a good time, and he railed against Moses. Compared to the hardship of wilderness survival, he longed for the security of enslavement. Such had been his lot for the previous 430 years.

Bondage versus Freedom

An interesting observation surfaces from the Hebrew's transformation from slave mentality to that of a free person: For the previous 430 years, during the passing of over twenty generations, someone else had initiated his daily routine and provided his food, clothing, and shelter. Supporting slavery's physical challenges had not built within the Hebrew sufficient moral character for him to support himself as an independent, self-reliant individual.

Without facing and conquering life's unending challenges, individual growth stalls. Personal progress may stop altogether, and this retardation happens to any group or individual denied the freedom or

---
64. Scripture: KJV, Exodus 1-15

motivation to secure life's needs, much less to pursue life's ambitions. Think of America's welfare state, of human beings virtually owned by government for government's purposes, not owned by themselves for their own purposes. Think of Socialism and Communism.

In each branch of Abraham's seed—Hebrew and Muslim—the distinction between a bonded mentality and a freed mentality came increasingly to bear as each branch moved through the centuries toward today.

Compare those of Abraham's seed who sought intellectual freedom to those whose dogma held them, and still holds them, creatively bound. Consider countries today that gasp at the recklessness of America's religious freedom. Consider those same country's contributions toward each citizen's upward mobility, economic and cultural refinement, and educational and scientific advancement.

The Character Process

Unable to found a society upon people raised in slavery, upon people never having connected survival to self-discipline, upon people never faced with producing all aspects of their own upkeep, Moses would keep his people wandering in the wilderness for forty years, giving the intellectually weak and complaining generation time to die off.

The lengthy travail eventually boiled Moses' followers down to a generation *taught in the way of the Lord*[65]—one that would exercise *justice and judgment*; one upon which could be founded a society with sufficient civil and moral discipline to give it a reasonable chance for survival, not to mention prosperity.

---

65. Repeated scripture: *"For I know him, that he will command his children and his household after him, and they shall keep the way of the Lord, to do justice and judgment; that the Lord may bring upon Abraham that which he hath spoken of him."*

The Ten Commandments

While the old ones raised in Egyptian slavery still lived, these malcontents indirectly caused a miracle to come about, and it did not work in their favor. Unable to tolerate incessant griping about hard times and bad food, Moses petitioned God for relief.

God relented and rained a daily ration of manna upon the wandering Hebrew, and sent coveys of quail to be harvested fresh daily. Since no one can attest to the taste and food value of manna, one may assume that it compares to whole-grain bread as quail does to meat generally. If ever a delicacy exists sufficient to tempt people into tramping mile after mile through briars of mesquite and cactus in a Texas hunt, quail is that delicacy.

Imagine being so favored by God that one's survival would be seen to in such luxury and detail. At the risk of his own life and with much effort and selfless dedication, Moses had freed his people from slavery and for them had found unlimited free food. One would assume that his followers would utilize their freedom and prosperity productively. Certainly, Moses believed that they would, but they did not. Actually, things went the other way.

Once his followers no longer spent the day hunting their next meal, they had a lot of free time on their hands. So, whenever Moses wasn't looking, they did awful things, not excluding much.

Now, in addition to incessant complaining bothering him, Moses became distraught over his people's behavior. Moses lost it, in a manner of speaking, and that's when God stepped in and helped him out again.

While on retreat on Mount Sinai, racking his brain in prayer for answers about what to do with his unruly mob, Moses was visited by God who saw fit to make a personal appearance. In rescuing Moses and in further support of His people, God introduced the Ten Commandments and more. With his own finger, God etched each word upon two stone tablets.

When Moses returned with the tablets, tablets written in doctrinal detail including the Ten Commandments and beyond, he found the people in such moral disarray that he smashed the tablets in frustration.[66]

Discouraged, Moses returned to Mount Sinai, and this time had to chisel another set of tablets himself. All he put upon the second set were the Ten Commandments. The wonders that God had put upon the first set of tablets, except for the Ten Commandments, were lost—at least for the time being.

During his frustration over the tablets God told Moses that if he could get his people to behave that he would make of them a great nation; that he would number them as with the stars of Heaven; and that the world would be blessed for and by their seed. Sound familiar?

Moses' blessing comes close to an exact replication of what God promised Abraham: namely, obedience and prosperity by promise, disobedience and tragedy by implication.[67] [68] And so it was with the Hebrew from the time of Moses until the reign of David.

Where Abraham had organized a few simple principles by which a person seeking a productive life should live, God, through Moses, added to the list, further refining what Abraham had begun. Though the tablet-smashing saga may have delayed the arrival of higher, more sophisticated law, at least the Ten Commandments and the accompanying Law of Moses[69] had been given. Moral technology had taken another step forward, intellectually strengthening Western civilization a bit more.

When one considers all that Moses faced in converting a wandering tribe with a slave mentality into a people capable of driving a

---

66. Scripture: KJV, Old Testament, Exodus 32–34
67. Scripture: KJV, Psalms 89: 30,31,32
68. Scripture: KJV, Leviticus 26
69. Scripture: KJV, Exodus, Chapter 21.

stake into the soil of civilization, his task seems overwhelming if not impossible. Consider how many tribes were wandering the globe during that same period, and then find one that compares to the Hebrews' transformation from nomadic wanderers into a civilized nation. How did Moses do it?

Moses did not do it alone. It was God who stepped in with an ingenious solution: He produced a list of standards of personal conduct that every person could understand and follow. God divided these principles into ten behavioral categories, each one selected for the effect it would have upon personal conduct, ultimately upon civil conduct and social order.

Now, no Hebrew could claim that he did not know to honor God; that he did not know to honor the Sabbath; that he did not know to respect his parents; that he did not know to manage sex; that he did not know to be honest and to respect human life. This religious—civil—code provided Hebrew society with greater societal structure than it had previously known, ever, or that any other tribe wandering elsewhere on the planet had come to embrace.[70]

Standards and Results

The plan worked because, following centuries of enslavement capped by forty years of useful instruction in the wilderness, the Hebrew, under Joshua's direction, at last occupied his promised homeland, and with David's reign some years later, came to prosper mightily. He thrived for a period beneath both the Abrahamic Covenant and the Law of Moses.

The Hebrew flourished as promised, settled in his homeland, and secured there by powerful personal and national character. Strength of

---

70. Consider the societies of Native American tribes, Bedouin tribes, Genghis Khan's Mongol tribes, Celtic tribes, Germanic tribes, Anglo and Saxon tribes, and countless others. Such tribes were ruled by the mightiest among them, not by law as Israel came to embrace. Did any advance to the degree of Hebrew influence still globally manifest today? Why not?

individual character had finally amassed sufficiently that a solid civil structure and powerful army could be built. But obedience to God's law did not last, and with it went character. With strength of character once again dissipated, captivity replaced freedom along with its accompanying prosperity and security. How many times did the Hebrew repeat the cycle of obedience and prosperity, and disobedience and ruin? Many, many times.

Jerusalem is a perfect place to live but seemingly impossible for God's chosen to securely maintain. Between the time of Moses and the time of Jesus, Egypt, Persia, Syria, Babylonia, and Rome[71] all conquered Israel but were only able to do so when the Hebrew was not following character-building law—law that when followed builds character sufficient to support independence.

When the Hebrew strayed from God-given direction, when he refused to uphold his side of the Abrahamic Covenant and the Law of Moses, a process that would have bound God to him,[72] he repeatedly fell into moral confusion, weakness, and bondage.

Obedience and Consequence

The consequence of obeying Judeo-Christian doctrine is a refined intellect accompanied by, and supported by, strong personal character. For it is strength of character that supports all aspects of an individual's life and the collective character of a nation's citizens that supports a nation.

While history solidly links Israel's societal success to moral character, the same linkage of morality to prosperity exists within every society today, within every home and family today, and within every individual life today, regardless of what spot upon the globe one calls

---

71. Listed are Israel's major conquerors. Innumerable periods of minor captivity also happened, and God sent a special liberator each time it happened.

72. Repeated scripture: *"I, the Lord, am bound when ye do what I say; but when ye do not what I say, ye have no promise."*

home. Neither a person nor a family nor a nation can avoid reaping what is sown; seeds of good fruit or seeds of something less.

Jesus, the Radical

In a further installment of the moral and intellectual technology that would ultimately produce the American Mind, Jesus came and finished what Abraham and Moses had begun. Jesus brought governing principles prophesied to fulfill—complete—the law.[73] His ministry saw him going about the countryside couching the Good News numerous ways, launching teachings about *moral agency*—choosing the right; about *repentance and forgiveness*—personal progress by putting away the past and focusing on the future; and about *going and doing*—a solid work ethic, from every angle imaginable.

Jesus advocated a switch in thinking so radical that few of his day grasped it, including local religious leaders even though they specialized in the topic. Jesus' new doctrine expanded personal standards from a theater of physical performance to include those of mental and emotional performance—from simply managing one's actions to managing one's thoughts, passions, and actions.

Jesus brought the hard doctrine but the rewarding doctrine. It is much easier to recognize the physical actions one *shalt not do* as contained in the Law of Moses than it is to eliminate unseemly thought. Consider the intellectual capacity proffered by accomplishing such self-mastery.

Consider Jesus' wording in this example: *"Ye have heard it was said by them of old time, Thou shalt not commit adultery: But I say unto you, that whosoever looketh on a woman to lust after her hath committed adultery with her already in his heart."*

Here, Jesus' new philosophy shifted behavior from deed to thought.

---

73. Scripture: *"Behold, I am he that gave the law, and I am he who covenanted with my people Israel; therefore, the law in me is fulfilled, for I have come to fulfill the law; therefore, it hath an end."*

Which is more difficult to accomplish? Which develops the mind, the home of character, the generator of personal talent and intellectual achievement, more?

How does Jesus' advice in the following scripture contrast with Man's natural instinct? How does it compare with Moses' *'an eye for an eye?'* *"But whosoever shall smite thee on thy right cheek, turn to him the other also."* And the famous: *"Ye have heard that it hath been said, thou shalt love thy neighbor, and hate thine enemy. But I say unto you, love your enemies, bless them that curse you, do good to them that hate you, and pray for them which despitefully use you, and persecute you."*

Political Threat

As Jesus' revolutionary ideal began attracting followers, His movement threatened powerful politico-religious authorities—Pharisees and Sadducees—their income in some cases and certainly their social standing and power.

The Pharisees and Sadducees of that day were religious parties not unlike political parties that we know in the United States today. And just like rival political factions wherein each group objects to views put forward by the other, in Jesus' case they combined to oppose his teachings entirely, and to kill him.

In the Israel of that day, like what Islam seeks in Sharia Law today, religious and civil law were one and the same. While religion is an affair of the heart—a most private affair, indeed—oversight of a nation's politics, including its economy, becomes many opposites: affairs of the politician's pocketbook; affairs of the politician's social rise; affairs of the politician's power and celebrity.

Except in the rarest of human hearts, the effect of celebrity upon reason and rationality emphasizes this point. Life ceases being about *we* and *us*, becoming instead about *I* and *me*.[74] According to England's Lord Acton, no human being can pull it off: *"Power corrupts, and absolute power corrupts absolutely."*[75]

Like what happens in many Islamic-dominated countries today, religious law in Jesus' period required citizens to observe vast behavioral detail or suffer severe consequences. For example, exceeding a set number of footsteps on the Sabbath was harshly dealt with. The offender could be bound and pelted with stones, stones the size of a fist.

Jesus had come to fulfill that unrefined code and replace it with one infinitely more expansive for the human mind. Unfortunately for Him, Jesus' new intellectual ideal—one that would eventually free religion from civil law in the United States—threatened those holding religious posts, and Jesus had to go.

To silence Him, those in power appealed to the Roman governor, Pontius Pilate. When Pilate found insufficient grounds upon which to execute Jesus, he suggested that Jesus' captors take him to their political leader, Herod.

Herod, a convert to Judaism and shrewd political leader, was empowered by the Romans to administer justice to all Hebrews. An occupational force in many countries at the time, the Romans allowed local politicians to administer local justice as far as local law did not conflict with Roman expediency.

While Herod's court dressed Jesus in a scarlet robe, crowned his head with plaited thorns, and mocked him as a false king, Herod withheld judgment and sent Jesus and his accusers back to Pilate.

To keep the peace, Pilate relented and allowed the Pharisees and

---

74. George Orwell's motivation to write his novel, *1984*, derived from witnessing corrupt politicians leading the opposition in Spain's civil war where field soldiers like him were wounded and died in filth and misery while their Communist generals drank champagne in elite hotels. This jolted naïve young Orwell from Leftist idealism to reality. He never saw life so innocently or naively again.

75. John Emerich Edward Dalberg-Acton, 1st Baron Acton, January, 1834–June, 1902, usually referred to simply as Lord Acton, was an English Catholic historian, politician, and writer.

Sadducees to have their way. He sentenced Jesus to death at their behest, washing his hands personally of the deed.

Incidentally, not long after removing the threat of Jesus, civil war erupted in Jerusalem fueled by growing animosity between the Pharisees and Sadducees, shattering the country once more. That's another story altogether but one that plays well today in many Middle Eastern countries where infighting between opposing Islamic factions, each claiming God's endorsement, continues.

Jesus died cruelly at the behest of powerful men but not before leaving behind a wealth of intellectual and spiritual technology that would not go away. As with Abraham and Moses, divine endorsement authorized Jesus throughout his teaching. He imparted that authority to the Twelve Apostles who were at his side while he taught. Through the sacramental ritual of *laying his hands upon their heads*, Jesus literally bestowed the same authority he had received from God upon the Twelve Apostles, making sure that his influence and authority would remain should he be absent.

The Struggling Word

Imbued with God's priesthood authority, and at the cost of their own martyred lives, the Twelve Apostles took Jesus' teachings around and around the Mediterranean region. During this missionary effort, the Good News found fertile soil in the minds and lives of simple people, not in those of high society, at least not originally.

His Good News appealed to people perhaps not educated enough nor sophisticated enough to reject the value of observing clear moral and ethical standards in making the right choices; of focusing on the hope of future goals and working toward their realization rather than dwelling upon past disappointments and grievances; and of displaying initiatives like charity, forgiveness, forward planning, and the unrelenting work ethic of *going and doing*.

Constantine and Nicaea

When Jesus arrived with his addition to what had come before, he affected relatively few souls as travel by foot, sailboat, or camel or donkey, were the principal means of carrying the Good News from place to place, and it almost died out.

Additionally, Jesus had been killed in the hope that his intellectual and spiritual initiatives would die with him, but they did not. His message contained principles too meaningful to be discarded out of hand, and many ardent believers, poor and without *purse or script*, dedicated their lives to its perpetuation. They did the best they could with communication being what it was. And, like Jesus, many were martyred in spreading the Word.

Following Jesus' death and the deaths of the apostles immediately at his side during the original presentation, many of Jesus' core teachings became polluted and confused. Though a few of the original Twelve Apostles were replaced when others were martyred, gathering a quorum to affect such replacements in times of difficult travel and impossible communication became unworkable.

The chain of priesthood authority eventually broke down and keys to and of Heaven were temporarily lost to mankind. But, because of the sheer richness, pragmatism, and explanatory doctrine of mankind's origin, purpose, and destiny, contained within Jesus' core message, it stubbornly hung on.

In 325 AD, Roman Emperor and newly converted Christian, Constantine, convened a conference in Nicaea, Turkey, of those employed by, or just dedicated to, spreading the Word. He sought a consolidation of Jesus' original doctrinal ideals through historical records.

As its most notable accomplishment, the Nicene Conference produced the first compilation of New Testament scriptural selections translated from Hebrew into Greek and later into Latin. The conference also created the Nicene Creed[76], the foundational doctrine of the Catholic church. This document contained theological definitions still observed today not only by the Catholic church but by most other Christian denominations as well.

To get everyone to go along, however, Constantine had to compromise some of Jesus' original teachings. The Nicene Creed resulted as Greece's pagan rituals became mingled with Judeo-Christian philosophy, bringing ritual and religion together in the minds of people not present three-hundred years prior when Jesus first presented the message in its pure and simple form.

Incorrect in many points and polluted with paganism in others, the doctrinal explanations produced at that, and successive conferences, exceeded what even the most imaginative mind might have conjured up. While these compromised doctrines found embodiment within the Nicene Creed, New Testament scripture remained relatively untouched. From that point onward, too, control of the Word fell into the hands of and was taken over by powerful men, pseudo-politicians in many cases.

Rather than Jesus' intellectual and spiritual advancement helping the average person improve daily life, ambitious men utilized the newly merged dogma to dominate ignorant nations. Common man would not regain access to the Message for another twelve centuries.

The Nicene Creed struggled, stagnating at the least and some say actually causing centuries of Dark Ages in the West. Even so, Jesus' revolutionary views had been given sufficient organization in New

---

76. The Council of Nicaea (325 AD) addressed—among other things—the issue of God's alleged *trinity in unity*. What emerged from the heated contentions of churchmen, philosophers, and ecclesiastical dignitaries came to be known (after another 125 years and three more major councils) as the Nicene Creed. These various iterations declared the Father, Son, and Holy Ghost to be abstract, absolute, transcendent, imminent, co-substantial, coeternal, and unknowable, without body, parts, or passions, dwelling outside space and time. With such a confusing definition, it's little wonder that a fourth-century monk cried out, *"Woe is me! They have taken my God away from me . . . and I know not whom to adore or to address."*

Testament writings to preserve their value to mankind until something better came along.

Chapter 10
Modern Architects – Luther to America

The Reformation

From the time Jesus' martyred blood sealed his mission of bringing purpose and direction to humankind, the next breakthrough for the Western mind came fifteen centuries later, in 1517, when a young German clergyman had finally had enough.

Like so many scientific, musical, philosophical, and technical marvels, that have originated in Germany, Roman Christianity came under the scrutiny of a bright, sincere monk. He rebelled, and his rebellion stood northern Europe on its head.

Nailing a list of objections to Rome on the door of the Wittenberg Church, priest Martin Luther outlined the deviant teachings that he believed had crept into cannon. Putting his life at risk, he stuck by his objections, publishing them in a series of freely available articles.

In a succeeding act of absolute defiance that put his life at further risk, Luther translated sacred scripture from Latin into German, and then, with the aid of a wealthy patron, sent the manuscript to be reproduced as a major project for Gutenberg's printing press. The book was then mass-produced and sold to anyone who could pay for it.

Back to the People

By making Jesus Christ's New Testament teachings available to all who desired to study them, Luther had reclaimed holy writ from elite theocrats—men often doubling as government officials and even politicians—and had given it back to the masses. There, as Jesus had originally intended, families were left to their own understanding of His teachings, not to have them filtered by professionals in foreign tongues or perverted by government officials or politicians whose income was too often proportionate to their management of the population rather than service to it.[77]

Luther's distribution of Jesus' teachings to Common Man liberated thought as nothing had before. Life began making sense. Learning how God sees things, and not how those in charge see them, reshaped human perspective. *Souls began to feel their worth. The weary rejoiced in the thrill of hope.* Rather than earthly passage being an exercise in drudgery and suffering, Jesus' teachings turned man's view of earthly travail into divine labor—labor not just for daily survival but focused upon personal intellectual, spiritual, and material progress. Conquering daily challenges now became a pathway to the eternities. Think of it: *Life's crucible now served to refine one rather than to grind one down!*

On behalf of the average person, Martin Luther had cracked open the door to Divine Purpose, and the German people exploded through the opening. But ahead of social refinement came waves of pent-up anger and resentment. Throwing off the bondage of intellectual repression, people knew they wanted more but were not sure just what more might be. What people did know was that they could now think

---

77. Note how this paradigm fits today's politicians. The politician's job is to get elected, there to bask in the prestige of elite privilege, celebrity, and income, that often accompany high public office, not necessarily to improve the life of the voter, though that is what he advertises. If the politician's job were to improve the voter's life, improvement would be measurable. Fifty years ago, the U.S. poverty rate stood at 14.7%. Today, it stands at 14.6%. For which political party do those at the low end of the economic scale vote?

freely. Would the next step be to *act* freely? What did that even mean? The very concept of freedom—liberty—was unknown, unimagined, having been hidden from them for centuries. Now that it suddenly appeared, they applied this new sensation to anything that resembled the dark authority that had held them subjugated for so long.

By the time angry mobs came to grips with their newfound freedoms of thought and action, a terrible rebellion had crossed the land, painting it blood red. As many as one-hundred-thousand Germans perished in the frothing.

It took years—about a decade—for peace to finally settle upon the fiefdoms that were to become the Germany that we know today. When calm finally settled in, universities sprang up; music and the arts advanced at rates unknown; and science, literature, medicine, politics, and economics, shot forward at blazing speed. Europe was off and running.[78]

The English Period

As a flourishing Germany led Europe into the intellectual future, England followed closely behind. The process of the average English mind observing progressive intellectual principles began around the year 1611 when King James, King of England, Ireland, and a portion of France, a lackluster fellow personally, changed the course of Western history as no English-speaking man had to date: Following Priest Martin Luther's example of ninety years earlier, he decided to translate the Bible into English and to publish the book.

Not to be outdone by the Germans, good King James had his version meticulously compiled from an already-begun English edition with a word-by-word, verse-by-verse, review from Greek, Latin, Hebrew, and German texts. Assigning Oxford's and Cambridge's most notable scholars to the task—forty-seven scholars in all—he desired

---

78. German rebellion: Approx. 1520–30.

that every home in England should have a copy. Holding to the belief that minds schooled in gentle Judeo-Christian doctrine would be easier to govern, the Crown subsidized the project.[79][80][81]

Free Thinking

It's doubtful that King James got all that he planned for because, once his subjects' minds became liberated by the Bible's progressive, activist beliefs and enlivened by its intellectual ideal, rather than becoming the gentle lemmings he assumed, with literacy and the New Testament's thought-provoking curricula, they blossomed into strongly empowered minds with opinions and plans of their own. As happened in Germany, a life of subservience was coming to an end in England. The people's voice was about to be heard.

Though James did not live to see it, coming decades of Englishmen began challenging everything they saw. Limited horizons were swept away by average minds pondering something other than how their next meal might be secured. Indeed, when they lay the Book down at night, sleepless because of some thought-provoking principle they

---

[79]. King James did not invent religious freedom for England. In 1563, forty-eight years prior to James assuming the throne, John Foxe published *Acts of Monuments of These Latter and Perillous Dayes*, known as the *Book of Martyrs*. In his work, Foxe chronicled the trials and executions of religious martyrs dating from 1375 through to his time. Foxe recorded barbarous acts committed by those in power against common men, men martyred for attempting to introduce holy scripture among the masses. Foxe's work had numerous editions, was widely read, and seeded the notion of religious freedom that was to be finally and fully established in America.

[80]. On October 6, 1536, a man was led from a dungeon in Vilvorde Castle near Brussels, Belgium. For a year-and-a-half, the man had suffered isolation in a dark, damp cell. Now outside the castle wall, the prisoner was fastened to a post. He had time to utter aloud his final prayer, *"Lord! open the king of England's eyes,"* and then he was strangled, and his body was burned at the stake. Who was this man, and what was the offense for which both political and ecclesiastical authorities had condemned him? His name was William Tyndale, and his crime was to have translated and published the Bible in English.

[81]. Prior to King James' efforts, cantankerous King Henry VIII (1491–1547) had Tyndale's English translation copied by a French printer soon after Tyndale's execution. The King then brought numerous copies to England where he placed them in key abbeys around the countryside, making them available to laymen to study at will. This exposure to raw scripture helped seed the Puritan revolution that was to come, and helped Henry wreak more havoc upon Rome by pulling Catholic adherents into his Protestant camp.

had just read about, juices rinsed through brains that never would have done so without this grand stimulation, a stimulation centered upon the difference between good and evil; between being progressively active or preserving the status quo; between acquiring particular intelligence or remaining coarse; between being a literal child of a loving Heavenly Father or simply one of the king's possessions.[82]

Fighting for Freedom

Good King James died in 1625. His son, King Charles, in trying to reverse the intellectual trend begun by his father, met his doom and was executed in 1649 by his own Parliament.

Historians describe the uprising against Charles as England's Civil War, referring repeatedly to the political influences at the time, but they miss the mark. A battle for religious freedom begun in Scotland sparked the controversy that eventually led to Charles' execution, and that forever changed the Western World.

Charles had wished a return to anciently scripted dogma. In opposition, the work-a-day Scotsman, now seeing himself as a child of God and not the property of some lord or state or pope, not only wanted to worship as he pleased but to live life according to the dictates of his own mind. Having felt the rush of his newly liberated mind, the Scotsman also demanded sufficient political freedom to discuss and to interpret life's panorama according to reason—his reason—as he had recently become accustomed. Since scouring his own Copy and experiencing the intellectual freedom to interpret its teachings as such unfolded in his life, he could not conceive of returning to the narrow existence previously expected of him.

Once out of the bottle, the genie cannot be easily put back. And this genie, it turns out, after freeing German and British minds, would

---

82. *We hold these truths to be self-evident: That all men are created equal; that they are endowed by their Creator with certain unalienable rights; that among these are life, liberty, and the pursuit of happiness . . .*

eventually find welcome residence in the American Mind. It has not left. In fact, it has bred its own race—an American race that will not go away either. As the Crown forever forward had to include the people—Parliament—in governance, American governance eliminated elite authority altogether—except God himself—depending directly upon the people, all people, common people, for its authority.

From England to America

By the time of King James' death, a little more than a decade following the beginning of his Bible project, half the homes in England possessed a Bible, and the English sprang to life. They read the Bible, as it was the first book mass-produced in England, along with emerging Shakespeare and, soon to appear, *The Pilgrim's Progress*. England's intellectual revolution repeated what had already happened in Germany with Luther's efforts but not with the accompanying violence, at least not until Charles' failed attempt to turn back the clock.

Within a remarkably short span, there emerged a newly literate portion of the English population espousing an intellectually expansive philosophy unlike anything known previously, a philosophy that tended each adherent toward becoming a better neighbor and certainly a more stimulating neighbor to talk to.

Simultaneous with prompting one to become a better neighbor, free-flowing Judeo-Christianity awakened within the same English mind an appetite for self-governance, a hunger only quenchable within a political environment where self-determination could happen. It was the soul's cry for freedom to self-determine, gleaned from holy writ, that fomented England's immense forward leap; not science, not political genius, and not economic prowess, as historians often credit.

The habit of personally exploring scripture in the home spread rapidly across the Isles, not unlike the explosion of the personal computer in the United States during the 1990s. As the most significant lead-in to all that would follow, King James' scripture pried open cloaked minds, allowing shafts of light to pierce the darkness and brighten horizons. It is here that the concept of liberty intensified in Western Civilization: *"Now that I know that I am a child of God and not the property of the state [kingdom], I must have the freedom to follow the path that God intends for my future. In fact, I demand the opportunity to pursue my future (and that of my family) as God and I determine best, not as the state determines!"* Life would never be the same in Western Civilization.

For two-hundred years following King James' gift to the English, the average person's horizon, which until that monumental turning point had been narrowly restricted to satisfying basic human function while serving a lord or the state [king], broadened remarkably. Forming the central text of familial study from 1625 until the mid-1800s, biblical profundities increasingly wove themselves into people's attitudes and ideas, and this was happening simultaneously on both sides of the Atlantic.

But space in England and Europe—religious and intellectual space for the not-well-born mind remained hopelessly limited. Being held prisoner by a political infrastructure tightly controlled by powerful families would no longer do. Because the average mind was expanding its knowledge base in a spiritually and culturally powerful way, something had to give; the Englishman could either fight back or leave.

Those who fought back on religious grounds suffered persecution, and lives were martyred as the old guard fought against change. This controlled atmosphere, along with trampling religious freedom, placed both intellectual and economic limits on upward mobility, thereby threatening the very survival of an intellectually progressive mind. Though rare exceptions did occur, the average person could only look forward to an average life, and average is not good enough for a mind aware that it's capable of far more.

When all was said and done, developed talent, high ethical standards, and a hardy work ethic—natural products of a free mind—had limited effect upon the life of England's common-born citizen. Out there somewhere, the vastness and virginity of America and tales of her freedom and opportunity held irresistible appeal.

The American Restoration

And so they left England, Europe, and other places. They came to America impelled by potent belief—belief inspired by Jesus' progressive ideals. They came fueled by righteous desire to a place where their dearest hopes could at last be mated with a compliment of law. They came believing that they were children of a loving God, endowed with the same rights enjoyed by any other child of God, including those of higher birth, including even the king.

This realization imbued them with worlds of self-confidence: Why would a just God have men arrive on earth civilly unequal to one another? Such thinking made no sense to anyone with even a modest understanding of New Testament doctrine.

Though much of Christianity's doctrinal detail had been mislaid prior to the Pilgrims' arrival at Plymouth Rock, a sufficient quantity remained, and America's revolutionary effort and eventual Constitution came to be founded upon those stubborn remnants. But life in America did not begin that easily for the immigrating Christian.

Civil Progress

Certainly, free thought and a place to freely exercise one's agency required some getting used to. As the forming society progressed, clumsy ideas like scarlet letters, witch hunts, and stocks in the public square had to run their course. But refinement continued.

By the time of the Constitution's drafting in 1787, sufficient sophistication had settled upon the land that the advantage of setting the mind truly free, especially setting it free from religious and governmental imposition, could be clearly seen. The United States of America became the first place on Earth where Judeo-Christian doctrine could freely run its course, and it did.

With the socio-Christian philosophies of England's Locke, France's Rousseau,[83] and America's Thomas Paine[84] guiding them, the Constitution's framers assembled Judeo-Christian societal creed into law.

In their Declaration of Independence from England, the framers opened their document by boldly stating that the *Laws of Nature and of Nature's God* had driven them to separation from England. By having their opening salvo acknowledge the Creator Himself, the founders clearly established *Him* as the force behind all they were about to organize, not themselves. From there, they went on to acknowledge *Him*, not the government they were about to institute nor the monarchy they were leaving as the ultimate grantor of civil rights.

When they later drafted the Constitution and soon after the Bill of Rights, in what might first appear a reversal of their Creator-based beginning, they conspicuously left religious oversight out of public policy.

Because the individual soul arrives on earth as one of God's creations, not one of the state's, government must be denied power over one's conscience. Nothing the Founders could conceive could be of greater value to the individual mind than complete ownership of all mental powers, conscience being the guiding compass for those powers.

---

83. England's Locke had been a priest before becoming a social philosopher and writer. France's Rousseau lived his teenage years with Jesuit Priests, and his resultant social thinking heavily reflected that influence. Both men, nearly one-hundred years apart, recognized man as God's creation, not government's, and believed that public policy should reflect this.

84. Thomas Paine's book *Common Sense* played a critical role in uniting the colonists against the Crown in a war of separation. Paine's basis was that people would be better off under law of their own creation than law imposed upon them by any authority other than themselves.

Government, they believed, should shroud religious conviction in highly protective walls, not regulate nor define it. So, they formed law protective of inspirational guidance, knowing that within the individual heart resides great power—the power to effect grand consequences.[85]

Self-Determination and Independence

Among all explanations of God's relationship to Man and Man's relationship to God, Judeo-Christianity's explanation prompts the most positive effect upon the mind of any known ideology or theology. While across the mind of every reasoning person tramps the *desire* to self-determine, to the Christian self-determination becomes *an absolute need—a moral imperative that even the threat of death cannot deter*. And few explanations define the American Mind better.

America's liberal founding finally offered mankind an abundance of freedom within which that impetus could be fully pursued. Until lately, with the rise of the American State in the elections of 2008, 2012, and 2020, America's very legal construct aimed at that purpose—to protect, promote, and empower the individual mind.[86]

America's Religious Garden

When Jesus presented his installment in Jerusalem—*when he fulfilled the law*—two warring politico-religious factions combined to kill him, hoping that his teachings would die with him. In stark contrast to what happened in Jerusalem seventeen centuries prior, a

---

85. Bill of Rights. First Amendment: *"Congress shall make no law respecting an establishment of religion or prohibiting the free exercise thereof..."*

86. Slavery abounded worldwide as far back as history can trace, as thriving within Native American tribes as within Rome, Greece, and virtually every other peopled spot upon the globe; the weak captured and indentured by the strong. In the West, Christianity was the only identifiable anti-slavery force. England's Christians put their foot down in 1807. It took America's Christians until 1854 to found the Republican Party, dedicated to stopping slavery's spread and ultimately to slavery's abolition. In the United States, a blood atonement of epic proportions had to be paid for slavery, and it was.

fertile garden awaited the American seeding. The American garden, revolutionarily fenced by liberal law was, and still is, vigorously tilled by the activist soul seeking the extreme of self-betterment proffered by setting one's own life compass and following its direction to a better life circumstance.

The wide-open religious environment contemporary to America's founding led to an unending stream of Christian varieties springing up. While non-Christian congregations also appeared in frontier America, the number of Christian denominations far exceeded others. With this vigorous seeding, a uniquely American restoration brought back all that had been lost or changed in the centuries following Jesus' martyrdom.

At long last, in America, a mind could freely embrace the totality of any doctrine it chose. Since Judeo-Christian doctrine overwhelmed any competing moral source, in a most literal sense, including forming the basis for America's constitutional strategy, Judeo-Christian ideals wove themselves into governmental policy as well as into the lives of everyday citizens.

Back to Basics

As Jesus had gathered his original clergy from among Jerusalem's laymen, most of America's post-constitutional clergy also came from the working class. Common men stood at the pulpit, untrained in ritualistic formalities yet approaching a level of spiritual understanding once possessed by the very disciples originally at Jesus' side.

Within America's liberal religious atmosphere, the same divine influence that had authorized the earlier dispensations of Adam, Noah, Enoch, Abraham, Moses, and Jesus, returned. Within this renewal, there reappeared every sacred principle, divine sacrament, and holy ordinance that had ever been visited upon the earth. Among these were the sacramental covenants of Baptism, of confirmation, of the

Lord's Supper, of repentance, of holy matrimony, of consecration, and of the laying on of hands for healing, blessing, ordaining, sealing, and setting apart divine callings.

Personal revelation also returned as part and parcel of a complete spiritual buffet. Notably encouraged within this reviving connection was the advocacy that each citizen form a personal relationship with God the Father—that they increase their knowledge of Him, His personality and character, and of His deep and abiding interest in each of His children's moral welfare and personal progress.

In a purely American event, religious pragmatism replaced Old World mysticism. Observed at the pulpit as well as within government, each accepted and was charged within its sphere to promote each citizen's onward and upward march. What sort of government would limit the growth of even one of its citizens?[87] What sort of Heavenly Parent would not prefer an environment wherein each child could maximize personal progress? With religious study advancing individual character and government advancing civic opportunity, what more could a soul require in answering life's purpose?[88]

A Natural Result

Truly it can be said after 240 years of piloting America that Judeo-Christian principles produce the most effective guide for a mind's intellectual expansion ever found on earth. As already mentioned, these key Judeo-Christian behavioral and performance standards now find themselves genetically embedded within American DNA. And the gene is this: *"I'll do it better tomorrow than I did it today. I'll be a better person tomorrow than I am today."*

---

87. The United States did not invent slavery; it inherited slavery from the British system. The Declaration of Independence's theme of "*...being born equal... endowed by God with unalienable rights*" gnawed sufficiently at the national conscience to cause the birth of the Republican Party, a political movement first to limit slavery and then to abolish it.

88. Socialism's perpetual failure is wholly attributed to its failure to recognize the Nature of Man: "*I must be free to determine my and my family's future. I demand that freedom!*"

Such has happened and continues to happen. Doing it better became and remains America's ongoing mantra. In addition to doing it better, being better—individual commitment to personal progress, to adopting improved spiritual, mental, and physical technology as soon as it is revealed or discovered—supersedes all else. To possessors of the American Mind, personal progress is a self-imposed demand, an expectation of self never fully requited, an actual gene pressing its possessor ever onward and upward.

As already noted several times within this work, from 1776 until today, carriers of this gene continue to meet, marry, and reproduce, populating the world with offspring loaded with ever-increasing portions of this potency. The curve of this genetic course appears generationally exponential, crowning each generation with talent greater than the previous one, pushing the probability that each American generation will outperform the previous one, and each has.

Taking a numerically comparative look around the globe, with only a tiny number of people bringing the American Mind to bear upon the world, the world benefits in standards of living never imagined even as few as fifty years ago. Historically speaking, fifty years isn't much.

Chapter 11
Religion and Character

God-based religion proposes, first, to explain man to himself and then to refine him. While different denominations approach these tasks differently, all measure a member's advance by that member's mastery of that denomination's behavioral tenants or commandments, which, according to that denomination, build that person's character.

But character as a paramount personal quality did not begin on the North American continent with the Christian Pilgrims, or with the Founders, or with the Boy Scouts. Character was important to native inhabitants long before Europeans ever showed up in their homeland.

Counted highest among assets that a young male Native American could possess was to be bravely trustworthy. In Plains tribes, initiation into manhood involved a stealthy raid—entering the tepee of a member of an adversarial tribe and returning with some artifact, the most prized being a piece of weaponry. Imagine the pressure a young man felt on such a mission.

For the deed to stand, verification took place when the article was returned to its owner in the presence of adult leaders of both tribes. So highly esteemed was this ritual that, even between hostile peoples, a truce would be called while facts were determined.

Once his character was established, the only way a man could negate it anytime afterward was to be caught in an act of cowardice or in a deception initiated by him that shifted circumstance or property in his favor. A single lapse in character could relegate the fellow and his family to ridicule and disdain, and at the extreme, to ostracism. Faulty character destroyed a fellow just as solid character elevated him.

William J. Bennett, in his compilation, *The Book of Virtues*, gathered timeless stories listing the effect of moral character upon the lives of individuals, upon group circumstances, and ultimately upon society. Boiled down, the principal consequence is that a person with strong moral character is dependable, trustworthy.

In ancient North American society, one's dependability and trustworthiness weren't just one's personal affair; the people in the next tepee depended upon everyone around them standing tall when the time came. Moral character and dishonesty and cowardice formed opposing forces in the survivability of an individual, a family, a tribe, and a nation. They still do.

The Worth of a Soul

God-based religion holds that a person's creation as an individual soul is a gift of God—the greatest gift of God. It claims that God formed man in his image and then gifted man to himself, make of himself what he would.

America's founders, whether professing belief in Jesus' divinity or not, were greatly influenced by this aspect of Judeo-Christian philosophy, the part that declares the worth of the individual soul.

Thus, the government they created facilitated each citizen's opportunity to optimize their destiny as an independent individual. Because character is key to this optimization, how and to what degree one's character happens matters, and matters greatly.

Judeo-Christianity versus Darwinism

With the exception of cosmic happenings, every worldwide and private event originates within a human mind. Since every human mind filters its decisions through its *worldview*, where one gets one's worldview and what that view happens to be matters. Fundamental to one's worldview, and the force that drives one's life most forcefully—pause and think about this—*is one's acceptance or rejection of Deity and, should one accept Deity, one's willingness to meet whatever expectation Deity might hold for one's life.*

It follows that each individual's belief about mankind's existence—God-based or not—combines with those of fellow citizens, and that becomes a nation's composite belief. This composite belief results in a nation's civic and moral personality.

In a tragic extreme, recall Adolph Hitler's deep and abiding embrace of Darwinism, a godless religion with no behavioral tenants beyond some arrangement between the law of the land and survival of the fittest.

Seeing the German race as the fittest among all human races to survive—mankind being just another species randomly evolving on earth—the Nazis began exterminating races they deemed less fit to survive. Think additionally of euthanizing physical and mental misfits among the Nazi's own German population also deemed unfit to survive.

Contrast Hitler's Darwinian plan for the human race—survival of the fittest by scientific design—to the design that England's King James wanted his subjects to consider. Contrast also the difference between the effect upon man that Darwin's view inspired in Nazi Germany to that of Him born in Bethlehem.

As these opposing philosophies nurture specific worldviews and resultant actions, which view encompasses the entirety of the human experience? What social attributes should humankind admire and emphasize? Should material gain trump charity, mercy, and sacrifice?

In projecting forward into the millennia that lie ahead, what form should mankind's worldview take? What would have been the ultimate result of Hitler's Darwinian worldview? How many races would the Nazis have finally eliminated in their drive to scientifically perfect the species?

Nazi Germany took Darwin's natural selection theory to its obvious conclusion for the human species. The Nazis saw their horrific actions simply as strengthening the species by selecting those it deemed fittest to survive, fittest to breed, and it was themselves—who else? Their efforts would have eventually cleaned up the human race, improving the species by survival of the fittest as they saw the process.

Years prior to Hitler gaining power, Charles Darwin was thrilled to learn that his theory had gained traction among German intellectuals. Charles did not live to witness the holocaust, nor the trial run a decade earlier in East Africa where German forces murdered whole segments of the native population.

While some Americans leaped into Darwinism, the American Mind did not. The distinction between the Darwinian worldview and that of the American Mind overwhelms. The American Mind looks back upon the Nazi period of *scientific racial perfecting* in horror and disbelief. Though not an exact parallel, abortion as a medical procedure resurfaces as science's view of life—not as a humane view of life and certainly not as a mother's view of life.

The horror of man's developmental process through Darwinian thinking spins the mind 180° back to Judeo-Christian thought, back to those tenants presented by Abraham, Moses, and Jesus.

Three Christian Pillars

In the presentation that cost his life, Jesus introduced three action items that facilitated intellectual—and civil—progress as never before. His method for strengthening the species far surpassed Darwinian technique, for it focused upon building man from the inside out, upon strengthening the mind by pitting it against itself in choice, not by who wins the fight—a charitable intellect replacing a beast.

Whatever one's worldview happens to be, personal progress follows and is inextricably tied to one's moral character, to the moral technology that instructs one's moral character. While other creeds have certain highlights, none drive, nor have driven, human progress to the degree of the moral technology begun by Israel's ancient prophets, fully and finally explained by the ultimate prophet, Jesus Christ.

Conspicuously identifiable within Jesus' vision for accelerating man's personal, intellectual, familial, and national development are the three behavioral guides, or the three paradigms for choice, already mentioned. Western civilization came to be founded upon these pillars, a process that triumphant individuals around the globe continue to embrace.

Tracking Jesus' three concepts of *moral agency*, *repentance/forgiveness*, and *going and doing* across centuries of development and implementation, consummation came, at last, in America with the American Mind being the result. The American Mind's behavioral sophistication had never been possible prior due to several inhibiting factors: Governmental intervention; faulty or incomplete Judeo-Christian doctrine or absence thereof; and people's inability or unwillingness to utilize Judeo-Christianity as an intellectual technology.

At its very inception, the American Constitution separated religion from government and did so for the protection of ideals held sacred by conscience, not for the protection of government as the American Left has lately popularized. Apart, Judeo-Christianity has historically outpaced competing intellectual technologies in advancing societal accomplishment among the masses.

To lesser degrees than within America, other Christian nations have progressed along. But, since no other nation availed itself of America's religious liberty and liberty overall, no other nation advanced or advances at comparable speed. Consider once again that not every religion acknowledges God—certainly not the God of Abraham, Moses, and Jesus.

In an accusation that causes one with a godless worldview great consternation, although claiming no religion, godlessness is the fiercest religion of all. Atrocities to lesser scales than what Nazi Germany perpetrated upon the Jews happened regularly as Western Civilization developed, but none endured. Tyrants appeared periodically, following godless paths similar to Nazism and they, too, vanished along with their cruel doctrines, vanquished in most cases by Christian blood followed by Christian light.

Fundamental, too, is that Judeo-Christianity's influence upon Western Civilization has lasted. It has persisted, founded and maintained upon Jesus' three character-building virtues—the first of which—moral agency—has already been covered. If unclear about moral agency, please review Chapter 4.

Pillar 2: Repentance/Forgiveness

While the first pillar in Jesus' intellectual technology, *moral agency*, pits choice against the highest-known ethical standard one can discover, the second pillar within his pragmatic construct is *repentance/forgiveness*.

Repentance/forgiveness puts away destructive, disappointing, or failed or obsolete behavior or technology in favor of a new start, a better way of doing it.[89] As soon as the everyday person got hold of Judeo-

---

89. In Dicken's *A Christmas Carol*, repentant Scrooge pleaded with the ghost of Christmases yet to come: *"Men's lives lead to certain ends. But if the lives be changed, will not the future be changed?"*

Christian scripture, people began trading an unproductive focus on past failures, grievances, and feuds, for the hope of something better in the future. In one of his most powerfully expressed mandates, the Author did not merely *suggest* that people forgive and move on, but he *required* them to do so certain of the effect that a free conscience and a mind free from hatred, spite, vengefulness, jealousy, and guilt, has upon personal progress.[90]

As the sixteenth, seventeenth, and eighteenth centuries passed, the abandonment of revenge's retarding influence brought about change—change that favored moving on, and intelligent minds did. Increasing numbers of minds began rejecting unproductive feuds and misbehavior with their accompanying feelings of guilt, grief, and dishonor, aiming their lives instead toward brighter tomorrows—tomorrows with new beginnings based upon moral choice, forward planning, and hard work.

The constant course correction mandated by *repentance/forgiveness* anchors both personal progress and technological progress. The principle reaches maximum potential when improved technology is proactively sought out and substituted for obsolete technology. And there are many technologies, Jesus' *moral technology* being the most advanced and meaningful among them.

The constant search for, and implementation of, better ways to do things—especially of observing ever higher standards for personal conduct—slingshots personal progress into the future with incomparable speed. Be it computer technology, business technology, medical technology, or moral technology, the ultimately successful mind actively seeks a better way. And, again, personal progress is the point.

Catastrophically evident among individuals or societies incapable of *repentance/forgiveness* is that they lock themselves into prisons

---

90. Scripture: *"I the Lord will forgive whom I will forgive; of you it is required to forgive all men."*

of stagnation—prisons of which they demand to be gatekeepers. By holding onto feelings of resentment, envy, hatred, revenge, or guilt, upon infinite repetition of non-innovative daily drudgery, upon resignation to a future devoid of hope, the thusly imprisoned soul denies itself the future without recourse. Life cannot move forward when focused backward or upon the same spot.

Consider also the challenge following misbehavior to admit to, to face up to, and to set right a wrongdoing. Just as damaging today as always, when a wrong has been committed it first appears easier to justify the action than to correct it, but that is not how life advances. Life is what it is; right and wrong exist. The cosmos cannot be reordered to call wrong right and right wrong simply because one has faltered or because one wishes that a wrong will go away. It will not, but it can be made right, and those injured can be restored.[91] In instances where a wrong cannot be fully made right, God has a plan in place to mitigate such a dilemma.[92]

Examples of Repentance/Forgiveness

In a brilliant display of *repentance/forgiveness*, consider the American Mind's response to cold-blooded impositions of one society upon another. Recall Japan's attack upon Pearl Harbor, the invasion of South Korea by Chinese-Communist-backed North Korea, the Holocaust, New York City on 9/11, and Europe following World Wars I and II. Consider the formation and defense of Israel. Think about families in endlessly warring Middle Eastern countries today.

Picture America in defense of herself and in defense of other wounded nations and peoples, at great sacrifice of her precious blood

---

91. Scripture: *"Do not suppose, because it has been spoken concerning restoration, that ye shall be restored from sin to happiness. Behold, I say unto you, wickedness never was happiness."*

92. Atonement: Reparation for a wrong or an injury. Judeo-Christianity holds that when reparation is impossible, Christ's atonement—through infinite anguish in the Garden and upon the Cross—pays that debt in lieu. One only need submit oneself and ask.

and hard-earned treasure, liberating and then rebuilding the homelands of both the victims and their attackers. Once that is done, the American Mind then becomes a sustaining partner to each. Name another nation with a similar worldview.

Pillar 3: Go and Do

On its way to building personal character, the third pillar wrought by Judeo-Christianity is the switch from *thou shalt not* to *go and do*, of an indomitable, forward-looking work ethic. While the previously mentioned principles—*moral agency and repentance/forgiveness*—provide structure and corrective guidance to the American Mind, this third aspect energizes the whole system.

Going and doing completes the journey from the Old Testament's rigid dictum of *thou shalt not*, from the letter of the law to the New Testament's charitable spirit of the law: *"Now, go and do!"*

Both concepts—letter of the law and spirit of the law—originated in Hebrew civil and religious history. The first from Moses' Old Testament and the second from Jesus' New Testament; the second testament founded upon and advancing the cause of the first; the second being more subtle and unquestionably more difficult to accomplish intellectually than the first; the second being a proven path to individual character, an expanding intellect, and unlimited personal progress.[93]

Triumph

Among life's many intrigues, exploring the subtleties of each Judeo-Christian principle makes clear how vitally important each principle becomes in producing life's joyful passage and outcome.

The effect these virtues have on spiritual, emotional, and intellectual development, even physical development, perpetuates—and

---

93. Poverty results from lack of ambition, from lack of industriousness, and from lack of self-discipline, not from lack of opportunity or resources, certainly when one finds oneself an American citizen. Too many cases make this point. What, then, does lift one out of poverty?

was designed to perpetuate—an improved daily product: Triumphant Man. No equal exists in that perpetuation nor will an equal likely be found.

Collect enough triumphant individuals within a home, and there appears a triumphant family, within a society and there appears a triumphant nation. In fact, enormous feats happen when just one of these individuals appears among men. Think of Jesus Christ, St. Augustine, St. Francis, Thomas Aquinas, King James, Joan of Arc, Martin Luther, Calvin, George Washington, Martin Luther King, Jr., Mother Teresa, and many others.

The names of many others will never be known because countless extraordinary people fulfill and have fulfilled the Judeo-Christian expectation, serving their families and communities in relative anonymity. Think of the world's mothers.

Chapter 12
Albert Einstein, Infinity, and God and Man

Jumping all the way from a discussion of religion to Einstein's theories and statements seems quite a leap, but it makes a point—perhaps *The Point*. And the point is about religion, about God and His design for humankind.

The physical universe's design demonstrates precision too exact for even the word *exact* to describe. Within a perfect framework of physics, chemistry, and quantum mechanics, a scientifically recognized force[94] set the course of science from the solar system's precisely orbiting planets to particles of atoms swirling within a molecule of water, and it did so in measures so definite that whole integers explain them—like $E=mc^2$.

Physical/Spiritual Science

While setting the course of earth's physical science, its inner precision of atoms and molecules and the solar system's outer precision,

---

94. Max Planck (1858–1947), the German theoretical physicist who originated quantum theory, saw intelligence in design the same way Albert did. His quotation: *"All matter originates and exists only by virtue of a force . . . We must assume behind this force the existence of a conscious and intelligent mind. This mind is the matrix of all matter."*

this Master Force had a purpose for such precision, and that was to prosper His spirit children as they developed. This He does by placing each spirit child within its own physical body—a *living* body. In support of that living body, this Master Force had to design a habitat that would enable not just human life but many life-forms. First on that list of life-supporting requirements was a dependable climate, hence the remarkable solar system with its miraculous sunshine. Next follows an abundance of water with its unique properties followed by a plethora of plants and an endless chain of creeping, crawling, swimming, and flying creatures, all dependent upon endless varieties of unseen but vital micro-organisms.

Paralleling the solar system's precise formation, the same Master Force put in place a precise intellectual system by which his spiritual offspring could grow and prosper and do so without limit. Why would such a Force not be thusly dedicated? Where is the logic in creating a human family, beings of such feeling, of such passion, of such noble potential, only to leave them without a great end and means to that end?

To Justify or Explain

Albert Einstein studied the world around him, searching for reality because truth interested him. He had the courage, even the desire, to seek out and embrace truth to such an extent that he spent time trying to disprove the very theory that had made him famous.

God, an ethereal concept not known to thrive in scientific laboratories, did not interest Albert early on. From what we know about him, Albert began life as an agnostic. The agnostic does not deny God; he simply says that since God's existence can be neither proven nor disproven, he chooses not to worship him—an intellectually honest approach.

But as Albert delved into science, as his mathematical probing led him deeper and deeper into the essence of matter, the precision that he discovered there led him to conclude that the world was no random occurrence. His quotes: *"I want to know God's thoughts; the rest are details"* and *"God does not play dice"* are two in a series of remarkably simple views of extremely complex subjects that define Albert.[95][96]

Albert's clear mind boiled complicated issues down into simple, short formulas, like $E=mc^2$. To state that energy equals mass times the speed of light squared appears simple, but days, months, and years were required to distill it, and at least that much time is required by even trained minds to understand its many implications. Ask the citizens of Nagasaki and Hiroshima, or the millions of people whose daily energy needs are met by clean, efficient, nuclear-generated electricity.[97][98]

The definitude uncovered in his mathematical explorations suggested to Albert that the cosmos could not be the product of chance probability. So, too, Einstein's unpretentious statement about learning God's thought process—the one great truth—contains much to ponder.

God and Science

What is *'is.'* What is *not* cannot be conjured up. No matter how much one would like to justify an action or supposed fact, if true principles don't square up, it's not going to happen. Correct principles are correct principles, and nonsense is nonsense.

---

95. Ibid

96. Albert Einstein: *"I believe in Spinoza's God who reveals himself in the orderly harmony of what exists, not in a God who concerns himself with the fates and actions of human beings."*

97. Speaking of nuclear energy: What about the sun? What about the sun's nuclear fusion that perpetuates forever? Who came up with that idea?

98. A kilowatt-hour is 1,000 watts used for one hour. As an example, a 100-watt incandescent light bulb operating for ten hours would use one kilowatt-hour. Nuclear-generated electricity costs $1.70/kwh to produce; coal $4.50/kwh, natural gas $$5.75/kwh, and wind and solar about $7.50/kwh to produce. As energy underpins the national economy, what should we do?

When Albert boiled away the fat, the basis for his scientific premise stood upon solid principles, irrefutable, the last fact in that scientific region; $E=mc^2$, and that's the end of it. Nuclear physics has proven it so.

God is like that. God is as absolute as any fact must be. His principles are absolute, too, because God's rules define science and vice versa. God's law and scientific law purely interchange; they are and must be one in the same. Truth happens when these two come together, real end-of-the-conversation truth.[99]

Since they are one in the same, the laws of science will catch you if the laws of God don't. That's what Einstein meant by expressing his desire to know God's thoughts and what he spent his life scientifically proving. His quest was not to find God through science, rather, the exactness that he discovered through science appeared too ordered, too precise to be randomly generated.

Moses felt the same way. So did Jesus. These brilliant Jewish men believed and proposed that with the same exactitude that God organized the universe's physical science that he also organized spiritual—intellectual—science, the detail of which is found in correct Judeo-Christian doctrine. And that is the reason for coupling these men in religion's concluding exploration.

As Einstein discovered the linkage of energy to matter, a string of biblical prophets linked man's character to the outcome of his life. Divine issuances like the Ten Commandments and Jesus' Good News mapped the route to intellectual and to character optimization. As Judeo-Christianity's orthodoxy refined itself across millennia, the harshness of Old Testament law—*an eye for an eye*—giving way to Jesus' New Testament doctrine brought the process full circle.[100]

---

99. Einstein: *"Science without religion is lame; religion without science is blind."*
100. Scripture: *"I have come to fulfill the Law."*

Chapter 12 * Albert Einstein, Infinity, and God and Man

The Science of Character

No mind becomes great in an instant but grows bit-by-bit, line upon line, precept upon precept. The process is not unlike the athlete that lifts weights, not to lift more weights, but rather to improve physical capability, to improve performance of a particular athletic discipline. The athlete has a goal in mind—the accomplishment of an ideal—and it takes a sense of purpose and a plan to get there.

As gravity pulling down upon the barbell creates resistance, it is overcoming that resistance, overcoming the adversity of the lift, that strengthens muscles. The amount of muscular strength eventually achieved depends upon the resistance of the weight being lifted and upon the lifter's courage and determination not to yield to temptation and stop the strain.

Like a weightlifter's will to improve athletic performance, each mind functions as an agent unto itself, able always to improve its intellectual substance. The level of substance acquired—spiritual, emotional, intellectual, and material accomplishment—depends upon honesty—objectivism—following God's laws, and hard work.

How does Einstein fit into all of this? The significance of a mind's development can be seen by repeating a comparison made earlier of Albert's Mind[101] to that of an average person. With a mind twice as productive as the average person who uses approximately 10% of their grey matter, Einstein, utilizing 20% of his grey matter[102] developed a formula to calculate the amount of atomic energy within a particle of matter.

If Einstein's discovery of the amount of atomic energy in a particle of matter resulted from utilizing only 20% of his mental capacity,

---

[101]. Years following his death, it was discovered that the left parietal lobe of Einstein's brain, though it had an average number of neurons, had significantly more glial cells—which produce and support myelin—than the average person's brain. At the time, the finding was considered meaningless. But now it makes perfect sense, bandwidth-wise.

[102]. Though debate rages on about the capacity of Einstein's brain, his ability to formulate thought—his power of deduction—clearly superseded that of the average mind.

what could a person do utilizing 100%? How powerful would thought become in such a fully developed example?

In a purely American view of what life portends, this describes God's intellect. And this is where each human intellect may arrive, provided it acquires all knowledge and has the courage[103] to make correct choices for a sufficient length of time.

If God exists and if the soul is eternal as Judeo-Christianity states, could the ultimate enlargement of the mind be *The Purpose*? Could the perfection of one's mind be the real enterprise taking place as one goes through life? Is all else happening around a person simply props on the stage that facilitate the play?

As a good actor does not let props hamper his performance, but support it instead, should the world be similarly utilized? While the world appears to be real, is it only illusory in developing the triumphant mind?

Focusing upon the simplicity and profundity of Albert Einstein, can one's mind accomplish in a particular field in a personalized way what Albert accomplished in nuclear physics? Could it be that one's mind—that one's heart—contains gifts and talents specific to it that are extraordinary; that will encourage the down and out; that will mentor the aspiring student; that will lift the forsaken or betrayed; that will comfort the aged and minister to the infirm; and that, most vital among all endeavors, protect, support, and encourage one's spouse and child?[104]

Is *your* mind willing to stand against forces that threaten its progress, the very ones that must be overcome for *your* ultimate fulfillment as one of God's children? Only God knows just how grand one's mind can become. Ceaseless learning, absolute goodness, and the courage

---

103. C. S. Lewis: *"Courage is not simply one of the virtues but the form of every virtue at the testing point, which means at the point of highest reality."*

104. Scripture: *"When ye are in the service of your fellow men, ye are only in the service of your God."*

of right decisions for a sufficient length of time—why would these not be His method for ultimate fulfillment? After all, an infinite universe requires infinite numbers of administrators, doesn't it?

Section 5
Standards, Challenges, and Examples

This section describes how Judeo-Christianity's *ethical standards*, more than any other factor, take the American Mind to unprecedented heights in terms of personal achievement.

This section explains how ethical standards, also known as *convictions*, function as first-line defenders against a mind's unavoidable exposure to such mental pathogens as licentious sex, drug use, pornography, gun violence, political deception, and corrupted history. It details how moral convictions keep the mind free to grow and to maximally serve its owner.

This section further explains how to make life better each day than it was the day before. It further explains how one's intellect can be cleaner, stronger, and sharper each day than the day before. It answers the question: *"What is tomorrow for otherwise?"*

This section takes a hard look at two of life's defining issues: sex and drugs. It concludes with a review of those American presidents who demonstrated just how valuable the American Mind can be whether on the world stage or within its own home.

Section 5
Standards, Challenges, and Examples

This section describes how American Instinctually's evident standards, more than any other factor, take the American Mind to unprecedented heights in terms of personal achievement.

This section explains how critical standards, also known as conscience, function as first-line defenders against a mind's unavoidable exposure to such mental pathogens as licentious sex, drug use, pornography, gun violence, political deception, and corrupted history. It details how moral convictions keep the mind free to grow and to maximally serve its owner.

This section further explains how to make life better each day than it was the day before. It further explains how one's intellect can be clearer, stronger, and sharper each day than the day before. It answers the question, "What is tomorrow for otherwise?"

This section takes a hard look at two of life's defining issues: sex and drugs. It concludes with a review of those American presidents who demonstrated just how valuable the American Mind can be whether on the world stage or within its own home.

140

Chapter 13
Standards and Character

When Boeing engineers set about building a jumbo jet—one capable of carrying hundreds of passengers across thousands of miles of potentially turbulent sky—they must end up with a dependable aircraft. This is where standards come in.

From the basic airframe all the way to the radar system that tracks storm clouds, skilled engineers design each aircraft component according to precise standards. Long before the aircraft lifts off on its maiden flight, long before it encounters its first threatening turbulence, any and every stressful load that might come to bear upon any structural component has been anticipated. Not only have the stresses been anticipated, but the structures that are to withstand the pressures have been tested and re-tested prior to being certified airworthy.

In application, Boeing engineers spend more time and money reviewing and implementing the standards that the components must meet than it takes to build the first aircraft that those components will produce. Once one group of engineers arrives at the standards that a particular component must meet, another group of engineers steps forward to enforce those standards during manufacture.

Following manufacture, it falls to yet a third group to assure that the standards the original engineers intended make it into the final product in their exactly prescribed form. Once united in the completed aircraft, the components are tested by still more engineers for dependability in unison, for the exactness of their coordinated response.

This is the science that makes air travel safe and affordable. It is a science of standards; standards being set, standards being followed, and standards delivering on their promise.

Standards function the same in human beings as they do in airplanes except the consequence of personal standards does not end when one deplanes. Personal standards become everlasting in their effects.

Aircraft Database

The Boeing engineer finds standards for his discipline in manuals, graphs, charts, and in enormous databases. Since 1903, when Wilber and Orville Wright scooted along the beach at Kitty Hawk and lifted into the air, detail after detail of manned flight has accumulated. Beginning with flight's most basic concept, countless trials and errors, countless failures and successes have formed a library of information about heavier-than-air flight.

As details accumulated over decades, sophistication increased with each aircraft iteration until commercial flight today is statistically safer than riding in a car. The process has been remarkable.

Intellectual/Spiritual Database

Descending from Adam's time until today, a similar process has been ongoing in developing standards that produce a fulfilling life. Think of the millions of examples of trial and error—of the millions of examples of trial and success it has taken to determine the standards that hold life on its most robust course.

Chapter 13 * Standards and Character

Should storm clouds lay on the horizon, an aircraft's radar system warns of their location and intensity. Human life seldom enjoys that same benefit. Opposition to personal progress lies in wait at every turn, often unseen, even camouflaged. That is the process of living, and that is the case for girding the armor of personal standards—convictions—about oneself and about one's family.

Personal standards anticipate threats to happiness, peace, and safety, and prescribe methods to meet and defeat such obstacles. Just as perfectly made aircraft do not assure cloudless skies, personal standards do not assure problem-free living. What moral, ethical, and performance standards *do* assure is dignity, self-respect, peer respect, strength of character, skill, peace, safety, personal fulfillment, and triumphant living.

Home: The Incubator of Standards

In the firmest foundation of any society, if each child were raised by loving parents that exemplify standards known to produce highly refined character, what more could a child require in gaining its best advantage in the world? And, since a nation's every citizen begins as a child, what would be the national result of such a citizenry?

In addition to a home wherein moral teachings thrive, where else are character-producing standards taught and learned? George Washington said, *"And let us with caution indulge the supposition that morality can be maintained without religion. Whatever may be conceded to the influence of refined education on minds of peculiar structure, reason, and experience both forbid us to expect that national morality can prevail in exclusion of religious principle."*[105]

George knew what he was talking about. Where do people go to learn the standards that produce truly refined morality, character's firmest prop? Every mind benefits from the regular reaffirmation of

---
105. George Washington, Farewell Address, 1796.

its higher purpose as a parent, friend, neighbor, provider, protector, nurturer, and child of God. Every mind benefits from a break from worldly chaos, a budgeted interlude outside of self that clarifies the processes by which life progresses most joyfully.

Of proven value is the standard of being in services at the appointed hour. From this comes renewed dedication to humility, to charity, and to spiritual history, culminating in a positive outlook, courage, confidence, order, reason, justification, understanding, hope, peace, safety, and purpose.

As already mentioned, some imagine that a God-based denomination robs them of freedom—of self-expression—and that having a denomination suggest one's standards makes one an automaton, a human robot. By implication, such minds deem themselves wiser than the combined knowledge of 6,000 years of recorded human history. Such an assumption naïvely misses the mark. A mind must select its ethical, moral, and performance standards and set them at will or the world will impose its standards instead. One's life is bound to the consequences of either choice.

Character is a Choice

Character is not a zero-sum game; reward may exceed input, but input must come first.[106] What is that input? Selecting and abiding by ethical, moral, and performance standards is that input. Since selecting and abiding by standards is a *choice,* building one's character is a choice. Since character begets happiness, happiness is the same choice. Since character begets accomplishment, accomplishment is the same choice. In reverse manner, unhappiness is a choice, too.

Solidly evidenced is that *a person devoid of loyalty to standards is necessarily devoid of loyalty to causes.* Unless a cause brings the selfish one to the center of attention, that cause is deemed unworthy

---

106. Scripture: *"For ye receive no witness until after the trial of your faith."*

of loyalty. Without loyalty to such causes as spouse, family, God, and country, what is left? What legacy awaits a life devoid of standards?

To produce the safest-possible aircraft, engineers select and follow the highest-known standards for aircraft production. To do less—to even consider doing less—would be placing passengers' lives at risk. What kind of person would do that? And yet, people do place their own and their children's happiness and success at risk by avoiding personal standards.

Memorable stories contain elements of extreme trial against the hero or heroine's standards, and then, by hardy, almost blind adherence to those standards, triumph and reward. Character trumping trial is what makes the story great. Without trial's defeat, there is no story. To every life comes trial.[107] That is the life experience. It is none other. What is life about, then, if not about trial's defeat and the joy that ensues?

Arland Williams

On a snow-driven January morning in 1982, a civilian airliner crashed into a bridge and fell into the Potomac river's ice-crusted waters. Not everyone died in the crash; a group of six survivors could be seen splashing about in the frigid water, trying to stay afloat.

Within minutes a Park Police helicopter appeared trailing a lifeline, a rope to which only one swimmer at a time could cling and be plucked from an icy drowning. Refusing to save himself until all others had reached shore, Arland Williams grasped the rope every time the helicopter returned to the river after saving one more life and tied the precious lifeline around another person. He first tied it around one person, then another, then around a third, a fourth, and finally around the fifth passenger in the group.

Each of the five trips to shore ate up precious minutes. With the

---

107. Jane Eyre, Charlotte Bronte (1816–1855)

passing of each minute, Arland's body lost more of its heat and strength. Finally, when it was his turn to be carried to safety, his strength was gone and he slipped beneath the icy water, not to resurface.

In a lasting tribute to standards—standards set and standards followed—Arland Williams reminds us of their profound value.

The standards that compelled Arland on that terrible but heroic day did not occur to him following the crash but began over twenty-five years earlier. Arland had been a Cadet at the Citadel, a military prep school in Charleston, South Carolina, and there had begun to adopt the standards that would not only govern his life but that would result in his final act on his final day.

Arland's character had already been *". . . determined by having made a thousand other choices in seemingly unimportant moments. It had been determined by all of the little choices of years past—by all those times when the voice of conscience was at war with the voice of temptation—whispering the lie that 'it really doesn't matter.'*

"It had been determined by all of the day-to-day decisions made when life seemed easy and crises seemed far away—the decisions that, piece by piece, bit by bit, developed habits of discipline or of laziness; habits of self-sacrifice or of self-indulgence; habits of duty and honor and integrity—or dishonor and shame.

"Because when life does get tough, and the crisis is undeniably at hand, when we must, in an instant, look inward for strength of character to see us through, we will find nothing inside ourselves that we have not already put there."[108]

Summary

Life's triumph is a matter of character, and character does not happen on its own. Character results from selecting and then abiding by ethical, moral, and performance standards. Since life can be difficult

---
108. Ronald Reagan (1911–2004), speech.

with or without strong standards, to face life without the intellectual power that standards produce makes no sense. Why not become the extraordinary person, the heroine, the hero?

An immense gulf lies between things *unpleasant* and things *difficult*. Hard work may be difficult, but not necessarily unpleasant. Upholding high personal standards might be difficult at times, but not unpleasant. However, a life weakened by inattention to personal standards can be unpleasant—unpleasant to oneself and unpleasant to dependents, personal and professional. And the contribution to family and peers of a hero's or heroine's life?

Examples of Standards

Language/Communication: Do you increase your vocabulary daily? Do you reference a dictionary upon encountering an unknown word? Are there words you refuse to say? If a second language is of interest, by what date will you be able to communicate in that language? What is literature to you? Are you discerning? Do you write? Do you read?

Education: To what level of education will you arrive? When? What subjects will you study? What grades will you accept? By what criteria do you select reading material? Name books that you read last year. Are you a better person for having read them?

Religion: Do you know what your actual religion is? Is God included or not? What do you believe about religion's three areas of pre-earthly life, earthly life, and the afterlife? If you accept God, do you wish to be in communication with Him? To which religious qualities do you aspire?

Morality: Are you honest with yourself and with everyone else? Are you trustworthy, loyal? Are you charitable, giving? Are there acts you refuse to perform? Are there images you refuse to entertain? Is your language clean, are there words you refuse to say?

Modesty: Is there clothing you will not wear? Are there exaggerations you will not make? Are there opportunities you will seek that allow you to encourage someone less fortunate, to grieve with the stricken, to empathize with the unfortunate? Are you humble, teachable?

Food and Nutrition: Do you discern what you take into your body? Are there foods or chemicals that you will not allow into your body? Do you know how your body processes different foods? Are there limits that you will and will not accept regarding your body's weight and fitness?

Personal Finances: Do you earn all of which you are capable? Do you look for opportunities to improve your career? Do you spend less than you earn? When will you be financially independent? Will you support charitable causes? Which causes?

Physical Conditioning and Grooming: Do you maintain a schedule of physical conditioning? If you compete athletically, what accomplishments will you meet and by what date? Does your weight match your body type and height? What body-weight limits do you accept?

Personal Presentation: Do you offer an easy smile? Do you quickly learn the name of everyone with whom you associate? Do you call others by name to validate them and personalize the relationship? Is your posture and bearing upright and cheerful? Is your hygiene proper? Do you dress better than the occasion requires, even at work? Is your clothing tasteful, modest, and clean? Is your hair neatly arranged and managed? Are your teeth clean, white, and straight? Do you listen to what you hear? Are you sincerely interested in those about you?

Chapter 14
Sex and Character

A force powerful enough to create life has to be mighty, and sex is that mighty force. Few human activities match sex in its ability to grip the mind. And like all human endeavors of great consequence, sex has two faces:

Life's joyful continuum shines in the first face with all the familial warmth that spousal bonding and resultant children bring to pass. In its face of glory, sex replicates the species in the wonder of children, and its powerful draw is pointed at that purpose. Connubial sex emotionally bonds two who have chosen to bring children into the world, bonding them sufficiently to see child-rearing through to completion despite life's periods of turmoil and hardship.

Cruel cankers disfigure sex's second face, leaving scars of betrayal, exploitation, lechery, treachery, lost innocence, dashed hopes, disease, filth, guilt, and vice. Sex's profundity is too great for any person to go outside sex's connubial domain and escape whole. On the contrary, those that understand and control this dominant human feature find controlling all other challenges comparatively simple.

Sex's Inevitability

Corn replicates in the field by pollen from male tassels dusting upon feminine silks that extend out of each budding ear. From outside the protective husk, the pollen magically makes its way inside the ear following the silk thread until it reaches the point where the silk attaches to the cob, and presto, a kernel of corn is conceived.

Every kernel of corn you have ever eaten came into existence this way. So did every kernel of rice, wheat, barley, oats, and, similarly, every blossom that led to every apple, pear, peach, plum, orange, strawberry, and so on.

Unlike corn's dusting of pollen upon the silk, the pollination of many plants requires a third party to transmit the pollen, usually an industrious bee looking for some nourishment to take home to its queen. And the queen bee, specially nourished to enhance her reproductive power, exists to mate, thereby replenishing her hive. She is female. She needs the male compliment to complete the cycle of her life. Without the masculine compliment, her hive dies out. Without corn's masculine tassel sprinkling its pollen upon the cob's feminine silk threads, the cob, the womb of kernels, shrivels. Each sex must play its part. As gender is eternal in DNA, the tassel is always male, and the cob is always female.

Sex and Custom

For every human being's age, mental capacity, and level of education, within all social mores and cultures, incalculable computations and permutations of the sexual experience play themselves out. Authors titillate readers about such things, deftly employing sexual intrigue, luring readers on page after page, straining to reach the moment.

But for all its forms and quirks, the act remains spellbinding. For that reason alone, for its power to grip the mind, to obsess the

Chapter 14 * Sex and Character

imagination, to attack volition, sex becomes an incomparable measure of integrity. The sex drive, judiciously and honorably channeled, crowns individual character as no other moral venue can approximate.

In Charlotte Bronte's classic, *Jane Eyre*, Jane's restraint of her passion for Mr. Rochester draws her into the reader's heart. She is admired and respected. Jane's strength in classical femininity is the most compelling feature of the story. Without it, there would be no story.

Bronte did not invent Jane. Such a person actually lived in Bronte's earlier England as the eventual wife of ruthless King Henry VIII. Disposing of his first wife by legal maneuver—Catherine of Aragon—and beheading his second wife for contrived infidelity—Anne Boleyn—he then fell in love with the young and appealing Jane Seymour. In pursuit of her, he sent a courier to her carrying a bag of gold accompanied by a romantic letter. Jane responded in a note that survives from 1536, instructing the courier: *"I pray you beseech the King to understand by my prudence that I am a gentlewoman of good and honorable family, without reproach, and have no greater treasure in the world than my honor, which I would not harm for a thousand deaths. If the King should wish to make me a present of money, I beg him to do so when God shall send me a husband to marry."*

They did marry, and two years later Queen Jane died while giving birth to their child. The king mourned her death pitifully. He could not be consoled for months. He would weep at the mere thought of her. King Henry had Jane buried with royal honors, and later had himself laid beside her.

Hollywood and the American Left can say all they wish about sex and shaking hands being one and the same. But it is not so and never will be. But the drive is there, and, where indulgence diminishes, appropriateness magnifies, dignifies, strengthens, and rewards beyond measure.

Societal Advance

Sexual self-discipline—do not read *inhibition*—rewards the family and strengthens a nation more than any known preparation. It always has. In direct anthropological correlation, a society advances or falters in direct proportion to its sexual discipline.

In a society where sexual mastery is not understood, where the sex drive is randomly satisfied among the population, the opportunity to strengthen personal character never happens. Such a society never strengthens. Intellectual and social stagnation, slothfulness, fatherless children, poverty, and disease, become chief manifestations.

As humankind flies just below the angels, not driven by wild animal impulse but by the cognizant choice of when and with whom one will be, inner strength accumulates to the judicious, strength to be called upon to bear up and to support the individual throughout life; throughout one's own life, that of one's family, and that of one's nation.

Another benefit of disciplined sex is *selection optimization*. Unlike an animal, instead of the female simply being covered by the male that wins the fight, discerning individuals consider partner traits such as honesty, loyalty, commitment to standards, respect for God, common goals, societal skills, education and income potential, family heritage, sense of humor, tastes in art and entertainment, devotional love, and moral discipline and character.

An even more selective participant might ponder qualities in offspring such as eye color, hair color, IQ, athleticism, disposition, and more. Mate selection among humans far exceeds what animals fight for because humans purposefully select what is best for optimum results, naturally.

The opposing sides of human selection—easy boys and girls giving in to each other, and discerning boys and girls demanding each other—foster opposing societal directions. Since the offspring of each group will likely supersede parents in either societal direction, this process contributes mightily to income inequality and to social and political polarity. A review of America's political constituencies shows just how wide this divide can become.

Sex and Abortion

America's Left fights hard to make abortion about women's rights. Yet, abortion is not about women's rights; it's about sex—irresponsible, self-indulgent sex. Removing the consequence of such sex does not reduce taking innocent life to a medical procedure. Killing is killing. Death is death. Abortion participants must ask themselves: *"On balance, was the sexual episode that led to conception worth taking the life of an unborn child?"*

A best-selling book measured crime statistics prior to and after abortion's legalization. The book concluded that increasing abortion correlated with reducing crime. Does anyone want to examine what this says about males who contribute to it and females who execute the process? Does eliminating sex as a character issue help anyone? Does it help a nation? Does anyone want to speculate on God's opinion?

Sexes' Physical and Emotional Origin and Tradition

In humankind's sex-determination system gender is determined by the DNA pairing of sex chromosomes at conception. A female happens when two of the same sex chromosomes (XX) pair up, and a male happens when two different sex chromosomes (XY) get together. Following genetic coupling, during puberty hormones complete the male/female distinction.

In this differentiation males have been sexual aggressors. Women, on the other hand, have retained ultimate sexual authority; the female must give permission. Here, nature places the decision in the hands of the one left with the result, hence, the one most qualified to make a rational decision. This is not good news for the aggressive, self-centered male.

From his disadvantaged position, something must be done to improve his chances. When the obligation of marriage appears too great a price to pay, trickery becomes the fallback option. Until the Sixties Women's Liberation Movement, such sly programs were individually produced. The Women's Liberation Movement challenged that age-old paradigm, elating men of a preying nature by seeing Woman lowered from her exalted position. Men and women are the same, aren't they?

What could be better news to an opportunistic male than having the female renounce her sexual authority? The man could finally, after millennia of facing resistance, be free to pleasure himself and then to move on—no guilt, no obligation. But the woman?

If aborting human life isn't painful enough for the woman to bear, being used and discarded, being left to raise a fatherless child leaves little to resurrect the mother's and the child's self-worth. Prisons teem with children of such beginnings.[109] Housing projects teem with such

---

109.
1. 63% of youth suicides are from fatherless homes (US Dept. Of Health/Census)—five times the national average.
2. 90% of all homeless and runaway children are from fatherless homes—thirty-two times the national average.
3. 85% of all children who show behavioral disorders come from fatherless homes—twenty times the national average. (Center for Disease Control)
4. 80% of rapists with anger problems come from fatherless homes—fourteen times the national average. (Justice & Behavior, Vol 14, p. 403–26)
5. 71% of all high school dropouts come from fatherless homes—nine times the national average. (National Principals Association Report)
6. Children with fathers who are involved are 40% less likely to repeat a grade in school.
7. Children with involved fathers are 70% less likely to drop out of school.
8. 75% of all adolescent patients in chemical abuse centers come from fatherless homes—ten times the national average.
9. 70% of youths in state-operated institutions come from fatherless homes—nine times the national average. (US Dept. of Justice, Sept. 1988)
10. 85% of all youths in prison come from fatherless homes—twenty times the national average. (Fulton Co. Georgia, Texas Dept. of Correction)

children and their exploited mothers. Poverty and low self-esteem are the child's signal inheritance accompanied by the mother's loss of hopes and dreams, or, if she didn't become a mother, the throw-away that abortion made her when she equated her special nature—creator of life—to that of a man.

Only the most unobservant would say that a woman's intellect, character, and innate value to society cannot eclipse that of a man, because it can and does—easily and often. But to say that men and women are the same requires an equally unobservant intellect. What degree of insecurity would drive a woman to abandon the special status that nature has assigned her since time began? Why would she want to be less? What degree of selfishness would drive a man to seek sexual gratification at the price of human life; the mother as a discarded sexual toy, the fatherless child facing a socially disadvantaged life, or a child eliminated as a medical procedure?

Intimate Treasure

Making love is aptly named for what the act accomplishes between a married man and woman. Married sex literally makes love happen between participants. Wholesome, God-ordained sex creates profound acceptance, trust, and deep attachment and affection between parents-to-be, between the two who will anchor the family—the two who must and will anchor the children's futures.

Good men respond to feminine virtue with a pledge of equal dimension; a worthwhile male appreciates feminine strength and quickly grasps the value of a lady of virtue. From the mating of two individuals of notable moral quality, the resulting family begins upon a foundation of granite rock. For with strength of sexual virtue comes strength in all other aspects of life. And these include principles of honesty, fidelity, faith, prayer, repentance, forgiveness, respect, love, compassion, work, and wholesome recreational activities.

In addition to the enormous benefit that sexual virtue is for the pair, the emotional development of their offspring to spring from individuals so strong and so honestly and purely connected cannot be overstated in value. Generations hark back to a defining couple—to the dedicated man and woman that changed their family's fortunes. It takes character to change the future.

Pinnacle of Marriage

In the sexual spectrum, starting at the top and descending downward where beauty and opportunity disappear, the marriage of a wholesome man and wholesome woman stands alone and unmatched at life's pinnacle. In this divinely intentioned union, the family becomes central to the greatest joy human beings experience. This joy happens two ways: In spousal bonding brought about by the act itself, and in deep emotional regard for one's spouse and one's posterity. Words cannot capture the depth of familial devotion and reward.

Sexual ardor heightens throughout the act between a righteous pairing because a trust-bound union frees the minds of lovers, unleashing heights of passion and emotion unknown in carnal attempts fettered by deceit, guilt, perversion, lechery, and non-commitment. When man and woman begin together following the ceremony, chains of tender niceties bind the innocent pair tighter and tighter, always leaving some fresh and exciting nuance for tomorrow.

When children arrive, selfless dedication spreads from spouse to spouse, from parents to child, and a higher plateau of love and meaning further enriches the union. Edwin M. Stanton, Abraham Lincoln's Secretary of War, courted and married the much sought-after Mary Lamson. He wrote her after their children were born: *"We years ago were lovers. We are now parents; a new relation has taken place. The love of our offspring has opened up fresh fountains of love for each other. We look forward now to life, not for ourselves, but for our children. I loved you for your beauty, and grace and loveliness of your person. I love you now for the richness and surpassing excellence of your mind. One love has not taken the place of the other, but both stand side by side. I love you now with a fervor and truth of affection which speech cannot express."*

Change of Terms

The word *'marriage'* used to have sacramental meaning, canonized within Christendom's Seven Holy Sacraments.[110] The word *'marriage'* used to affirm the sanctity of life; the word *'marriage'* used to affirm the noble use of the powers of creation with spouse and of co-creation with God; the word *'marriage'* used to affirm the solemn responsibility of man and woman to care for each other and to care for the children. The term *'holy matrimony'* now means what the word *'marriage'* used to mean.

Holy matrimony between man and woman affirms the eternal, complementary roles of gender; the father to preside over the family in love and righteousness and to provide for the necessities of life and the protection of his wife and children; the mother to be primarily responsible for nurture of the children. And nurturing new life is no small matter. No greater contribution to mankind exists than the product of loving parents.

No child asks to be conceived, and to be born. Rather, each is invited by Mom and Dad to join them in life's great adventure. Thus, every child is entitled to birth within the bonds of holy matrimony, and to be reared by a father and mother who honor marital vows with complete fidelity. This is life's supreme accomplishment. This is supreme family intimacy. One need only hold one's newborn to know that this

---
110. When the Supreme Court was considering the civil rights of same-sex couples, lawyers representing the petitioners were asked by judge Antonin Scalia if being granted civil union status with every legal right accorded traditional couples would suffice. The petitioners said no; they must be accorded the word itself: *marriage*. Again: The basic tool for the manipulation of reality is to change the meaning of words.

is true—and to hold and be held by one's faithful companion during life's many storms.

Strength of Character

Among the notable tenants of Eastern religion is its concept of *pure potentiality*. This field comprises all life's possibilities, ranging from the highest to the lowest. Self-dominance moves one upward in the field and yielding to weakness moves one downward.

The Christian sees the same essentials; righteousness is up to Heaven, and sin is down to Hell. One need not recognize religion at all, Eastern or Western, to see the same directions in human lives resulting from sexual choice.

Definitions of success vary, some toward spirituality, others toward materialism. It is rarely materialism that surfaces in the eulogy. For, from upon the shoulders of a single stalwart pair, of a man and a woman of determined sexual character, spring multiple generations of offspring, students, and disciples. It often takes the same number of generations to recover from sexual misuse. Unequivocally, among all character venues supporting life's joyous advance, God-ordained sex knows no equal.

Chapter 15
Drugs and the Mind

A second challenge of great and grave consequence to the mind is presented by mind-altering drugs. Whether ingested as a food like fructose in an apple or caffeine in a cup of coffee, life is best managed when the effects of various chemical elements upon the mind are understood and mastered.

The human body depends upon food for the energy that powers muscles as muscles move the body about. Food is the fuel that heats the human body optimally to 98.6° Fahrenheit. The body depends upon food for cell replacement, tissue development, and the many other chemical and biological reactions and processes that support life.

The amazing human body can pull off these functions on any number of vastly different foods. In old Ireland, potatoes formed over 80% of the average person's daily diet. On little more than potatoes, multiple generations of Irishmen produced succeeding generations of Irishmen, each happy and healthy.

Rice did and does the same thing for the Chinese that potatoes did for the Irish; that corn does for many Mexicans; and that blubber from whales does for some Eskimos.

Potatoes, rice, corn, and blubber do not contain the same ratios of the same vitamins and minerals, nor do they contain comparable amounts of starches, fats, sugars, oils, or proteins. But the human body efficiently processes what it is given, and given the most basic of foods, it survives, adapts, and finally prospers.

The observation is that the human body prospers in innumerable dietary circumstances. Not only does the body prosper on varying menu selections, but feelings of contentment prosper as well. Bear in mind that these feelings may not be connected to a single menu item. This may be bad news to chocolate lovers, but marvelous news to Sherpas in Himalayan scarcity.

Good nutrition amounts to nourishing the body sufficiently to sustain itself in good physical health and emotional contentment while living out the measure of its existence. Such a realization questions the many claims made about what should be eaten. In the cases of the Irish, Chinese, Mexicans, and Eskimos, perhaps it isn't what they eat, but what they don't eat that matters most.

Nourishment Plus

Besides just eating to stay alive, everyone longs for more. People everywhere long for the occasional tasty zinger, and if that zinger ramps up feelings of well-being, all the better.

Long before Columbus set out to find a cheaper way to get pepper, people around the globe had begun processing spices, stimulants, and other items that created special tastes and sensations, and selling them to their neighbors. No one knows who processed the first poppy or who decided to roll and fire up the first tobacco leaf, or who ground peppercorns into dust fine enough to cover a roast, but businesses blossomed as soon as the discovery was made that pleasure beyond a full stomach existed, and that people would pay dearly for such an experience.

Sugar High

Dietary pleasure beyond a full stomach occasionally gets out of hand. During the sixteenth and seventeenth centuries, the English became dependent on sugar. The blast that sugar brought to daily drudgery blew weary eyelids wide open and lit the afternoon teatime. Sweetened tea became the order of the day, and an order it was and remains.

To the astonishment of American soldiers storming Normandy's beaches on D-Day, in the midst of flying bullets and exploding mortar shells, at the appointed hour British soldiers stopped everything, sat up makeshift tables, brewed some tea in their helmets, dumped in packets of sugar, and sat there calmly sipping. True enough, pleasure as a necessity becomes an addiction.

Addiction

The seriousness of an addiction depends upon several factors: financial cost, health implications, productive downtime, and collateral damage. The cost of daily tea and sugar for the British is relative: To the poor, sweetened tea is an expensive habit. Its price is nothing for the rich.

The health implications of sugar aren't so simple. They begin with dental considerations—such as rotten teeth. And while causing teeth to decompose, sugar makes people fat. In perhaps its most damning effect, sugar interferes with mental function, actually altering personality, even upsetting the outcome of a life.

Within a few years of Columbus' discovery of the tropical West Indies, the natural environment for sugar production that he found there prompted the development of sugarcane plantations. Of the two groups of natives occupying the Caribbean Islands—one of peaceful vegetarians and the other a group of fierce cannibals—a viable labor force for sugar production could not be raised among them.

None too excited about being eaten by their workers, the enterprising plantation developers decided to avoid the locals in favor of an imported labor force.

First in mind were the Irish, and a few boatloads were brought over to give them a try. Since the Irish weren't keen about leaving their Emerald Isle in favor of sweating away in the tropics, they were impressed and brought against their will: slaves. But tropical diseases like malaria and yellow fever soon decimated the Irishmen, and replacements had to be found.

As it happened, African kings were selling fellow countrymen by the boatload—and at very low prices. One only had to send a ship to Africa, and it would be immediately loaded with human cargo. Additionally, the African was believed tolerant to malaria, yellow fever, and most other tropical plagues. It didn't take long to make the switch. Within a short span, boatloads of manacled Africans began arriving in Hispaniola.

Collateral Damage

The collateral effect of England's centuries-old sugar addiction was a slave population in the New World, a population of fractured African families displaced halfway around the globe. In their most reflective moments, when the King and Queen sat down to tea, they had no idea what their habit cost in human terms—costs born from the 1600s until today and beyond.

From the time sugar became available to common people until today, what has been its accumulated health cost? Start by totaling the pain endured from rotting and lost teeth, a virtual plague until this century. Before antibiotics and modern dentistry, when colonized decay reached the tooth's nerve portion, infection set in. The pain was excruciating. Infection lasted for days and sometimes weeks as a pustule of yellow puss formed around the roots of the bad tooth in a face swollen to half again its normal size. Swimming in this fetid pot, the tooth would eventually loosen and could be pulled out or even spit out.

Raging fevers accompanied this process from beginning to end, weakening the body throughout its fight against infection. Undergoing such stress with each decaying tooth—and they became infected in a succeeding chain until there were no more—death often resulted. Fever and sickness easily overpowered an immune system weakened by battling tooth infection. Even childbirth and the common cold during such battles could mean death.

By thirty years of age, few people in sugar-eating societies had any teeth at all. Poor health and shortened lives resulted not only from the battle with tooth infection but from the inability to properly chew nutritious foods like meat. Americans count beloved George Washington among this group.

Listing sugar's further effects, obesity and its tragic ramifications must be included. Today, one-in-five American adults carry over one-hundred pounds of fat lumped upon their skeleton and marbled throughout their muscles. In addition to a struggling self-image, add diabetes and its devastation of bodily organs, overtaxed backs, hip joints, knees, and feet, to high sugar intake. Not only does the body fall apart under the load of sugar-resultant fat, a bloodstream constantly loaded with sugar eventually produces feelings of victimization as sugar chemically interferes with serotonin production.

Serotonin

Serotonin is the brain chemical that creates a sense of relaxation, a sense of well-being, of peace, of purpose. Serotonin influences self-control, impulse control, and the mind's ability to see beyond the moment and plan ahead. Serotonin aids in achieving deep sleep, a point of mental relaxation necessary for optimum intellectual renewal and clarity.

Depression, including clinical depression, finds its miserable effect deepened by low serotonin levels, most often the result of consistently high blood-sugar levels. When depressed, the sugar-addicted brain craves sweets or the similar carbohydrate structure of alcohol.

Satisfying these cravings becomes a core goal, generally unrecognized and denied, but a central focus still. And the sugar cycle is vicious enough just with serotonin's connection to depression, but there is more. A second brain chemical whose production is also diminished by sugar's constant presence in the brain is beta-endorphin. This immensely powerful chemical raises sensual perception to extreme levels of intensity and does so naturally.

Beta-endorphin

Beta-endorphin produces the highest of highs. Beta-endorphin can be ten times more effective than morphine. In its absence, emotions drop to feelings of depression and deep victimization. Self-esteem drops from existence, replaced by desperate cravings for relief, relief easily found with more sugar.

When sugar's effect diminishes, sugar's first cousin, alcohol, waits in the wings as the next most powerful beta-endorphin replacement. The conclusion that sugar wreaks havoc upon personal productivity and happiness can be easily made.

Beyond User Damage

Like other mind-altering drugs, enormous peripheral consequences have followed sugar all its days. How about incorporating into the sum of sugar-related grief the timeless agony of displaced and abused slaves and corruption from their trade?

In 1807, England outlawed slavery and slave trading, but trading in products produced by slave labor kept its place in the empire. To appease its mercantile conscience, Parliament passed laws encouraging both ships-of-the-line and those of privateers to confiscate slave ships bound for the Americas[111]. But ships loaded with the products of slave labor continued finding their way safely to the Isles. Like most political issues, the question of slavery became compromised in another collision of morality and expediency.

Certainly, in the United States, the effects of oppression linger. They linger among Whites who liberated slaves during the bloody Civil War only to witness their government's continued holding of African-Americans in perpetual poverty through failed welfare policy. Unending rows of newly constructed public housing filled with single mothers tell the tale.

Slavery's effects linger within the hearts of African-Americans from their fractured history, from being brutally captured and sold by their own countrymen, from inhumane treatment by their purchasers, and from an unending struggle for social acceptance, self-respect, and self-worth. Imagine being held today as the slave of a Leftist politician, exploited for Leftist political power? And all of this begun for want of a zinger, a bit of sugar.

Beyond Sugar

Because life is seen through the peephole of each mind's limited worldview, it takes a bit of pondering to gather the tiniest portion of what might lie beyond one's immediate cultural doorstep. Hardly anyone knows or thinks about the effect sugar has had on world history, much less the effect it has had and continues to have on the individual mind, even one's own. And we're talking about something very simple: Sugar. Cheap, legal sugar.

Few drugs fill history as does sugar, but the pattern set by sugar overlays most other abused substances. For want of a feeling of

---

111. Slaves were Africa's chief export from the fourteenth century until the eighteenth century—brothers and sisters captured, manacled, and loaded onto slave ships for a price. African slave markets were owned by, sponsored by, and profited from, by fellow Africans.

escape, a fake emotional lift, life can take off in directions tangential to a circle of happiness. Knowing that the sought-after high is fake, the unfulfilled mind goes after it anyway, courage and diligent resistance be damned.

Nicotine and Caffeine

While nicotine and caffeine may not rot teeth or make one fat as does sugar, both substances, in addition to giving false senses to the brain, contribute to the body's physical deterioration, ultimately leading to premature death, cancer being their killer of choice.

But sugar, tobacco, coffee, sugared soda and energy drinks, are legal, and lives suffer plenty from them alone. Who needs more? Some do. Some go to great lengths to do drugs that are not only illegal but dangerously harmful. They seek a higher high, a distance ever further from the reality of their lives. Such trips to never-never-land have multiple components: One of going away; one of coming home; and others of a more tragic nature. While a hangover is alcohol's homecoming party, and a diminished lifespan the endowment of sugar, caffeine, and nicotine, even more misfortune awaits one returning from marijuana, heroin, methamphetamines, fentanyl, Prozac, Oxycontin, and more.

When the marijuana user lights up, the tragedy spurred by the economy of their pitiful indulgence cannot be evaded; they must consider their part in lives lost daily in drug wars, prison sentences, and overdose deaths.[112] Responsibility for their part in the corrupt and senseless culture of mind-altering drugs must be borne by the user as well as the pusher. Personal responsibility for collaboration by both buyer and seller cannot be rationalized away.

Adding marijuana to the list of approved mind-altering drugs like

---

112. Legalizing marijuana does not lessen its position as sentry to the drug gateway. If getting high is the goal, how high is high enough? And, when it's all over, what did the high do for you?

alcohol is a fool's mission. What's next in line behind marijuana? Meth? Heroine? Fentanyl? Removing a person from a ghetto will not change that person's life until the ghetto is removed from the person. Standing against life's difficulties instead of hiding from them beneath a cloud of marijuana smoke is the *Answer*.

As with all standards that support a prosperous life, the forward-looking individual draws a line regarding the intake of any mind-altering chemical. Without a line drawn, without conviction, without a behavioral standard, without a clear distinction among options, one's life may and will wander from its most productive and happiest path. Tomorrow will come after all. Welcoming and meeting it head-on with courage and skill, again, is the *Answer*.

Life's Ups and Downs

There once was a grizzled old cowboy who had known hard times and good times. He had seen floods wash away portions of his herd. He had seen killer droughts when his herd had little grass to graze upon. In bad years, he had taken his herd to market but could not sell them because no one had money to buy.

He had traveled to town with those unwanted herds, slept in boxcars, eaten cold beans from a can, and returned to his ranch in the same clothes in which he had left with barely enough money in his pocket to survive another year.

He had seen good times too. In good years, he had also traveled to town to sell his herd. While in town in good years, he had stayed in the best hotels, eaten the finest food, and danced with the prettiest girls, kicking the heels of shiny new boots high into the air until the wee hours. In the good years, he had ridden home on the fanciest saddle cinched to the best of horses, his saddlebags filled with gold.

When the time eventually came that the cowboy stood before Saint Peter and the good saint asked him to sum up his earthly experience prior to entering through the pearly gates, the response came: *"I've been up and I've been down. I like up a lot better."*

Even though the old cowboy suffered from circumstances beyond his control, he also prospered from circumstances not fully of his making and to similar degrees. But for the *up* that he so preferred to exist, for it to be measured and appreciated, *down* had to exist as well. Conquering life's downs rather than hiding from them is another among the many rich inheritances of the American Mind.

Chapter 16
Presidential Examples

American presidents become subjects of intense scrutiny. Much can be learned from studying their presidential tenure as well as their whole life. Of particular interest here: How did the American Mind paradigm covered in this book influence their leadership? We will not cite presidents absent the American Mind, but it's not hard to name them.

George Washington, Father of the Country

George Washington was the very model of what the American Mind was to become. In any analysis of his life, it is seen that he was rationally self-interested. His rationality stemmed from Judeo-Christianity's guiding principles governing his life throughout, and such a worldview brought equanimity to his view of and service to his fellowmen.

His feeling of moral obligation can be seen in loyalty to his wife and family, and in loyalty, respect, and kindness to those around him. He honored the nation he was building. He honored political friends and foes. He honored soldiers serving under him. At Valley Forge and other places, he sacrificed with vision, yielding ease in the moment with a vision of a better tomorrow. His work ethic surpassed those around him with the possible exception of his aide-de-camp, Alexander Hamilton.

Washington was the only one among the seven slave-holding founders to emancipate his slaves. His will provided for freeing his slaves upon the death of his widow, Martha, but she freed them within a year of his passing.

Andrew Jackson, Old Hickory

If you've ever tried to break a hickory branch across your knee, you know the toughness from which Andrew Jackson drew his nickname. He had to be tough to face all that fate dealt him. Jackson's parents were Irish immigrants. Jackson began life fatherless; his father died while he was still in the womb. His two older brothers died from wounds suffered in the Revolutionary War, and his mother perished soon thereafter, worn down by caring for wounded soldiers.

These misfortunes cast young Andrew into the home of a relative with whom he soon proved unwelcome. At the tender age of thirteen, life threw him upon his own devices; sink or swim; live or die. He chose not only to live but to dearly grasp life and all that it might offer. Part of what life offered was self-respect, an attitude gained by learning and mastering codes of honor—those codes embedded in the Bible and absorbed in secular form into southern society.

He killed an offender of his name in a duel. After the opponent, whom Jackson allowed to fire first and whose shot hit Jackson in the chest, with blood draining down his body and filling a boot, Jackson coolly raised his pistol and shot the man dead. He attacked another who had slandered the name of his beloved Rachel. From these and other skirmishes, Andrew Jackson entered the White House carrying two pistol balls lodged in his body, each a testament to his sense of honor.

Chapter 16 * Presidential Examples

When wife Rachel died between his election and inauguration, Jackson remained just as true to her memory as he had been to her person. During his presidency from 1829 through 1837, slave interests in South Carolina threatened to tear America apart. The Union had to be and would be preserved and defended. Jackson held slaves, yet, when it came to the Union, he objectively subordinated personal interests to those of his fellow citizens. His unflinching, uncompromising resolve backed down South Carolinians who had been threatening nullification of congressional edict, even threatening succession.

Modern critics of his slave-holding interests and harsh treatment of Native Americans were not present when those issues dominated current events, daily challenging a president who was a human being charged with leading a budding nation, one that was fighting for its very survival.

Like Lincoln who followed him into the presidency thirty years later, Jackson read whole chapters from the Bible regularly; he claimed to read three chapters daily. Lincoln referred to Jackson more than to any other person in forming his rationale for prosecuting the Civil War. America would not have had the Lincoln it did were it not for Jackson's example.

When Jackson perceived that eastern monied interests in a central bank would usurp financial autonomy from the American people, he defeated them, single-handedly standing for what turned out to be the right course. To him, the people came first—congress, lobbyists, and special interests be damned!

Taking a cue from Washington's behavior toward his men during the Valley Forge ordeal, Jackson was impeccably loyal to his soldiers during the War of 1812. He was loyal to his friends, his wife, his wife's memory, his family, and his nation, the citizens of which he assumed as family. Consider the view a stern father would express toward his family, and contrast that with today's groveling governmental leadership. How might the children turn out in each case?

According to legend, a visitor to Jackson's plantation—the Hermitage—shortly after Jackson's death asked one of Jackson's slaves whether he thought that the general had gone to Heaven. *"If the General wants to go,"* replied a man who'd known Jackson well, *"who's going to stop him?"*

Speaking in Philadelphia in 1848, historian George Bancroft said of President Andrew Jackson, *"Before the nation, before the world, before coming ages, he stands forth the representative, for his generation, of the American mind."*

Honest Abe, Martyred Abe

But among all presidents including Washington and Jackson, Abraham Lincoln reveals greater portions of the American Mind than any other. Reviewing his self-written speeches, he could also have been the most intelligent. His deference to honesty, to humility, to loyalty, to vision, and to hard work defies comparison.

No legacy beyond preserving his nation—the home of the American Mind—need be built for Honest Abe. In holding his country together, no president endured on a daily basis, and with hardly a moment's reprieve, a more torturous tenure than did Lincoln. Despised by half the country and belittled by the other half, he marched on undeterred in preserving his nation and all that it portended for mankind. Observing a chronology of photographic images during his presidential service, life can be seen draining from him, making him old from unsupportable burden—burden from which he did not shrink. And he sealed his efforts with martyred blood.[113]

Irrepressible Teddy

The American Mind's most exuberant example, Theodore

---
113. Scripture: *Greater love hath no man than this, that a man lay down his life for his friends.*

Roosevelt, took the American Mind to places it had not been. At home, Teddy felled formidable trusts one-by-one, freeing working families and the nation's economy from their grip. Having no tolerance for the trusts' threat to the American Mind, he broke them into little pieces. When Congress and special interests resisted, the sheer force of his character came to the front, and he triumphed.

He had no tolerance for foreign powers interrupting his American Mind's plans either. Teddy sent the Great White Fleet around the globe, demonstrating that the American Mind had arrived. With gusto, he marched his own American Mind down to Panama, never hesitating to cause revolution and mayhem as he ushered in the American Century. When Bolivia resisted his Panama Canal proposal, he supported a revolution there that fostered the birth of the Republic of Panama. Unlike today's apologists, he didn't care if others aligned with his purely American view or not.

Like Lincoln and like Jackson, he knew where he wished America to go and would not be deterred from taking her there. Teddy recognized no global test. In his ready opinion, no society promised that which his beloved America offered to the future. Why align your fortunes with people going someplace else? His American Mind was incapable of entertaining any compromising posture; the American Mind had places to go, and he intended to lead it there.[114]

The Middle-American Mind

Harry Truman possessed the American Mind in a fashion unknown in the midst of eastern elites since fellow mid-westerner, Lincoln, had walked among them. Emerging from the shadow of Franklin Roosevelt, Middle-American Truman knew the American Mind; it was himself.

---

114. Editor of T.R.'s quotational biography, Mario R. Di Nuzio, titled the book, *Theodore Roosevelt: An American Mind*.

During his years of fame, he picked up none of the elitism so contagious in high places. Harry was grounded in the solid roots of his mid-western American Mind and remained grounded in them until the end. Throughout his life, Harry remained as precisely loyal to his family as he was to the cause of liberty.

Though elevated by a political machine, Truman remained his own man—and a real man to the degree possible in politics. When asked to admit special favor, he complained and resisted. He equated holding political office to fiduciary public service, not to personal celebrity and gain. During the buildup to WWII, his duties varied from consoling narcissistic politicians to defending the public trust through the oversight of defense contractors, and he excelled at both.

Charged with the unparalleled weight of using mass destruction to end WWII, he stepped up. After making the decisions of Hiroshima and Nagasaki, he bore the consequences without flinching; America and the lives of American boys came first. There was no hedging and no guilt. Regret never disturbed the sleep of Harry's American Mind.

Moments after Dwight Eisenhower took the oath of office and Harry was no longer president, he and Bess got into their Pontiac sedan and drove home to Missouri. No fanfare, no military escort, no secret service; just he and Bess returning home together, two American Minds enjoying one another's company.

Recent Example

Ronald Reagan possessed great quantities of the American Mind. A decade of exposure to General Electric's capitalist model moved Reagan's mind from liberal to conservative, from global to American. Exposure to market realities—to the process of securing economic prosperity for American families—replaced the wandering liberalism he had observed as president of the Screen Actors Guild. Once hired by GE as its celebrity representative, it didn't take him long to grasp the same vision held by GE's industrious American Minds—those bent on delivering into any American home that wanted it a lifestyle exceeding that of any other country.

To the dismay of the American Left, Reagan exposed and crushed enslaving communist doctrine whenever and wherever he could. The conscience of his American Mind permitted no other course. When a liberal Congress embraced the Soviet and Cuban-backed, Daniel Ortega, and attempted to thwart Reagan's effort to free Nicaraguans about to fall under communist oppression, Reagan and his associates defied the order. Risking political injury, even imprisonment for some of his co-collaborators, movements behind the scenes supported Nicaraguan freedom—freedom in the American mold, not life in the Communist Soviet mold, nor life in the timid mold of congressional progressives.

Reagan's adamant Americanism came ultimately to bear in Reykjavik, Iceland, in October 1986. In the American and Soviet disarmament summit held there, Gorbachev became convinced that Reagan's American Mind could not and would not compromise; Reagan's every fiber cried out against the slavery of Communism. His American Mind, against the advice of his own State Department, demanded the defense of republican democracy. The Soviet Union, already on the brink of economic ruin, collapsed soon thereafter.

The Absolute

The problem with an absolute is its stubbornness; an absolute does not change to suit the moment, it cannot—neither a scientific absolute nor an ethical absolute. An absolute would not serve science nor mankind if it were changeable; the game cannot be won if the goalposts are constantly moving about.

While elitism scoffs at moral absolutes, Reagan's American Mind, like Truman's, Teddy's, Washington's, and like Lincoln's and

Jackson's, fully embraced the absolute of America and the absolutes of her Judeo-Christian founding—namely, the U.S. Constitution as absolute, biblical commandments as absolutes, and God as *The Absolute*.

Jackson referred to the holding of these absolutes as *stubborn virtue*. To be sure, the American Minds just examined all exhibited and clung to stubborn virtue. Elites call this perspective quaint when being kind and stupidly uneducated when expressing how they really feel. The danger incurred when not recognizing and adhering to moral absolutes is, as our beloved Yogi Berra stated: *"If you don't know where you're going, you might wind up someplace else."*

Final Thought

When alone with one's thoughts, one's hopes and aspirations come to mind. Destiny lays in wait, but how will it turn out? What will make the difference between a good ending and a common or bad ending to one's life? The determining factor between a good outcome and a poor one is the way one thinks—how one's mind processes its surroundings. No formula for living ever visited upon humankind comes close to doing for the human life what the American formula does. Millions of American Minds have not only achieved their dreams by this method, but millions have exceeded what they thought possible when beginning their quest.

It is true that God supports the righteous desires of a clean heart. However, that statement is incomplete: While humbly *deferring to God's will,* one still must do one's part by vigorously applying principles of *objectivity*, *moral agency*, *repentance/forgiveness*, and *going and doing* to one's life. That is what does it.

Additional Points to Ponder

A decades-old Hollywood production makes a point, though accidentally. In a scene that tears one's heart out, performed by the superb actress, Emma Thompson, whose husband has just betrayed her. When her husband took off his coat upon returning from work, she notices a small box in an inside pocket. Snooping, she discovers a gold necklace, her Christmas gift.

Monitoring a box of the same size under the Christmas tree, she chooses it as the single gift each family member gets to open on Christmas Eve. To her horror, the box she opens contains a CD of old Joni Mitchell songs, not the necklace. The necklace had gone instead to her husband's mistress, a young girl at the office.

Emma is seen standing by the couple's empty bed, sobbing over the discovery. While she is undergoing this torture, everyone else in the movie is either immersed in premarital sex or happily involved with someone other than their spouse.

When a male character's best friend marries, the young man begins carrying a torch for his buddy's new wife. He persists, and she eventually rewards his attention. In another scene, an unmarried couple spends time together naked, getting to know each other, eventually getting engaged, and everyone is thrilled for them.

Another young man in the movie travels to a foreign country to bring back a tattooed and pierced trophy for himself and another for his friend. The men are overjoyed with their catches.

The last couple of interest includes the Prime Minister making it with his maid, a foul-mouthed pudgy girl who has just abandoned her live-in boyfriend because he treated her with disrespect.

In a rousing finale, the Prime Minister picks his maid from all which a Prime Minister could choose and carries her away to bliss.

It's hard to distill the message.

Life as You Like It

Assuming there is a message, does it suggest that one can have life as one wishes it to be, like ordering a hamburger at Burger King®, fixed the way you like it?

Life's realities cannot be ordered as one would like them to be. In real life, the future cannot be demanded. In real life, the future is ordered with choice. Choice begets consequence and consequence becomes the future.

While consequence may approach what is hoped for in choice, the future's strict conformity to an intended consequence can never be demanded. Ask a cancer victim or a spouse whose mate has broken sacred vows.

So, when ordering the future with choice, from which basis does choice derive? Choice derives from core values, righteous or not, acknowledged or not, personally selected or not. And what element forms the basis of one's core values? Religion. Whether or not God is included in one's religion, it is religion as defined in this book that forms the basis of everyone's core values. And this fact does not go down easily with those whose choices have not taken them to the best place.

From this book's earlier definition of religion, everyone has a religion whether or not God figures in or whether one acknowledges religion as an aspect of one's life or not. A biographer can help a great deal in explaining the choices and consequences of his subject with an intimate exposé of his subject's deference to the Almighty, or absence thereof. Seldom is the influence of Darwin's godless view mentioned in describing Nazi atrocity, while the fact remains that godlessness lay at the very heart of National Democratic Socialist Germany.

Such analytics must happen because identifying worldviews that produce happiness and prosperity and pointing out those that do not supersedes any other point that this or any other narrative may make.

Man, Science, and the Cosmos

Cosmic order is just as fixed in spiritual/intellectual science as it is in physical science, and order cannot be rearranged in either category to suit the moment. Spiritual science cannot be rearranged to answer an individual's misdeeds any more than physical science can rearrange Newton's laws of motion or Einstein's theory of relativity. The law of gravity is here to stay and so are the spiritual—behavioral—laws that lead one to happiness, prosperity, and safety.

Those who struggle against this analysis wish this reality would go away. It will not. Again, physical science and spiritual science rely upon absolutes intelligently designed and built into the cosmos. Pitted against these absolutes, choice is justly answered in consequence—intended and unintended. Added together, these consequences accumulate to become the future; that of one's personal life, of one's family's life, and of one's nation's life.

The Guiding Pillars

Human life succeeds best when choice is based as near to reality as can be determined in the moment. In whatever circumstance it finds itself, the American Mind *objectively* filters choice through the Judeo-Christian paradigm of: 1) *moral agency*—choosing the right, choosing according to pre-determined moral standards, standards tested and true; 2) *repentance/forgiveness*—discarding useless, failed, or obsolete behavior or technology in favor of a new start, a better way of doing it, and granting others the same opportunity; and 3) by *going and doing*—anxiously engaging life through an indomitable work ethic that challenges adversity through to domination.

It is by constantly adapting behavior to this humble formula that the American Mind has accomplished for mankind all that it has and why it accomplishes for the individual all that it does. Why has this formula been effective? Why does it continue to be effective, surpassing all other processes for personal advance?

The Judeo-Christian formula for living excels because it drives the mind to never rest in its quest for an ever-higher plateau of understanding, of performance, and of being. Think once again of the victim of terminal disease or of any seemingly unearned misfortune. Calamities occur. When they occur to the American Mind, the new struggle is immediately dropped into the Judeo-Christian matrix for trial. Life thereafter moves onward and upward once more, to a higher plateau still. This is *The Process*.[115] This is the science of life, the meaning of life, the reality of life—a reality dictated by material and spiritual absolutes. The future bows to this approach with positive predictability and will continue to bow for history proves it so.

Paraphrasing Einstein once more, *"God does not play dice."*[116] God is not whimsical, and neither are his standards for behavior.

---

115. Scripture: *"And we know that all things work together for good to them that love God, to them who are called according to His purpose."*

116. Einstein: *"Quantum mechanics is certainly imposing. But an inner voice tells me that it is not yet the real thing. The theory says a lot but does not really bring us any closer to the secret of the 'Old One' (God). I, at any rate, am convinced that He does not throw dice."*

Excellence in physical science and excellence in spiritual science are bound by irrevocable[117], immutable law.

The Odds of Darwinism

It has been computed that the number of random mutations required to produce the human optic nerve from a puddle of water surrounded by mineralized rocks surrounded again by a gaseous atmosphere is an exponential number that spreads across 41,000 zeros. This calculation makes the random mutation of lifeless minerals, gases, and water into the human optic nerve a mathematical absurdity.[118] The same sort of absurdity surrounds those who ignore spiritual science in terms of producing the comprehensive mind.

Attacking life's trials and goals objectively through the Judeo-Christian ethics of moral agency, of repentance and forgiveness, and of going and doing exceeds any competing formula for human growth, prosperity, and happiness.

Those civilizations acknowledging this ordered prescription prosper. Those societies that ignore or abandon these cosmic statutes struggle, and many have ceased altogether. Too many examples tell the tale.

Once more to Einstein: We know that he enjoyed genius sufficient to mathematically satisfy himself that the order of nature was not accidental, was not the result of random happenstance. He found nature to be supported by Reason[119].

---

117. Scripture: *There is a law irrevocably decreed in Heaven before the foundation of the world upon which all blessings are predicated. And when we receive any blessing from God, it is by obedience to the law upon which it is predicated.*

118. Researchers Hoyle and Wickramasinghe produced this number. To grasp the enormity of an exponential number extending to 41,000 places, one must know that the total number of atoms in our solar system is contained within an exponential number extending only 80 places.

119. Albert Einstein: *"I am satisfied with the mystery of the eternity of life and with the awareness and a glimpse of the marvelous structure of the existing world, together with the devoted striving to comprehend a portion, be it ever so tiny, of the Reason that manifests itself in nature."*

Einstein's colleagues corroborate this view, making a person's declaration of atheism just as absurd as has become Darwinian's postulate of the origin of species. If species advance from form to form, what was the first species? Where did the life energy come from that energized the first species? What are the current intermediate species? And, what will be the ultimate species?[120][121]

Like a mini solar system, the particles swirling in an atom hold their orbits exactly. In earth's solar system, if the earth or any other planet in the solar system minutely changed its orbital path, gravitational equilibriums would falter, the earth's orbit would change, and radical weather would remove life from earth.

The same Reason to which Einstein deferred, placed and maintains the earth in its precise spot in the solar system, not chance. And deference to spiritual science holds the soul in place, not chance, and certainly not the opinion of some New Age intellectual.

Good and Evil

No one appreciates someone who is uppity. Few welcome a scolding, even when it could make things better. But good and evil do exist, and the soul's development happens in a medium between the two. Refined character develops in no other way than choosing between these opposites and making the best choice that can be determined. No one gets the laws of Nature or of Nature's God the way one would like them to be.[122] The cosmos cannot be reordered to suit the moment.

Nature litters life with trial, and adherence to reason carries the soul through it. In life one moves toward the light or away from it.

---

120. The agnostic takes the respectable position that since God's existence can neither be proven nor disproven, logic dictates a neutral position on the matter. The atheist, by definition, makes the untenable claim that God does not exist. Laid to either arrogance or stupidity, such a claim cannot be proven and so has no basis either in science or logic.

121. Please read, Meyer, Stephen. C.: *Signature in the Cell; DNA and the Evidence for Intelligent Design*, Harper Collins, 2009

122. Nature's God as a reference, Declaration of Independence, 1776

This is the contest in which all human beings find themselves. The American Mind loves this light. That is how it came into being in the first place, in humankind's quest for life's meaning. In a move prophesied by the Ages,[123] the American Mind formulated a government that facilitated light's societal employment and its employment in every mind in every home.

Because some degree of light is ever-present, it warms no matter how dimly seen in the moment. It draws. It heals. It is real, and a mind's application of the Judeo-Christian matrix makes its full brilliance attainable. It is not by fluke of chance nor by magic that such potential arises. It is by justice—justice that rewards rather than justice that penalizes. Know this: Justice *will* happen. Reality will track you down!

Who Cares?

It has been estimated that at the time of the American Revolution that only 12% of the population supported breaking away from British rule. If this is true, then what was going on in the minds of the 88% that did not become involved? Were they simply willing to toil life away on the King's behalf rather than on their own behalf and on behalf of their family? Were they willing to accept life's outcome as government dictated it to them, not unlike what today's Progressives seek to reimpose? What about one's intimate plans, hopes, dreams, and aspirations for one's future and those of one's children?

Freedom's Worth

"If we believe nothing is worth dying for, when did this (Ronald

---

123. Scripture: *"Wherefore . . . a promise, that inasmuch as those whom the Lord God shall bring . . . shall keep his commandments, they shall prosper upon the face of this land (America); and they shall be kept from all other nations, that they may possess this land unto themselves. And if it so be that they shall keep his commandments they shall be blessed upon the face of this land, and there shall be none to molest them, nor to take away the land of their inheritance; and they shall dwell safely forever."*

Reagan gesturing around the Rhode Island state house as a symbol of the American Republic) *begin? Should Moses have told the children of Israel to live in slavery rather than dare the wilderness? Should Christ have refused the cross? You and I, my young friends, have a rendezvous with destiny. If we flop, at least our kids can say of us that we justified our brief moment. We did all that could be done."*

During Ronald Reagan's time as an ambassador for the General Electric Corporation, he took a break between appearances at General Electric plants to tour the Rhode Island State House. While there, he ran into a group of schoolchildren who were touring as he was. As Reagan was a recognizable celebrity, the children's teacher asked him to speak to her young, impressionable students. The preceding is a quote from those remarks.

Search Reagan's words a second time. Surely, he intended his remarks to inspire the children. With that as his goal, what thoughts could possibly have crossed his mind that prompted him to link a government building with life and death? What to him would make the subject he spoke of so extreme?

Approximately one century earlier, Lincoln had drawn inspiration from men who had died for something they believed was worth the price: *". . . we cannot dedicate—we cannot consecrate—we cannot hallow—this ground. The brave men, living and dead, who struggled here, have consecrated it, far above our poor power to add or detract. The world will little note, nor long remember what we say here, but it can never forget what they did here. It is for us the living, rather, to be dedicated here to the unfinished work which they who fought here have thus far so nobly advanced. It is rather for us to be here dedicated to the great task remaining before us—that from these honored dead we take increased devotion to that cause for which they gave the last full measure of devotion—that we here highly resolve that these dead shall not have died in vain—that this nation, under God, shall have a new birth of freedom—and that government of the people, by the people, for the people, shall not perish from the Earth."*

Lincoln spoke these words in Gettysburg, Pennsylvania, on November 19, 1863. On the first three days of the previous July, 51,000 American casualties had occurred in the fields over which he spoke. He had come to commemorate their sacrifice. He had come to inspire others about freedom's value and price, and to draw inspiration himself from that bloody event.

To Ronald Reagan, the Rhode Island State House symbolized what democracy—his republican democracy—offered mankind. But just what was it about his republican democracy that caused him to equate its value with life itself? What are the roots of such a view of one's republic, the same view that the soldiers of Gettysburg died for, and that Lincoln died for? Do today's generations value that view as did Reagan and Lincoln? Do today's generations even know what that view is much less how and where it originated?

Answering Reagan's question to the schoolchildren along with the sacrifice of Gettysburg that Lincoln commemorated—ultimately sealing with his own martyred blood—requires a search back in time that traces many centuries of development. It's a journey that concludes with the ultimate product of Reagan's and Lincoln's mutual republic: The American Mind. Without the American Republic, the American Mind would never have come into being. One invented the other. One produces the other. One depends upon the other.

A Worthwhile Quotation

When Moses was apprised of his impending death, God pointed Moses to his assistant, Joshua, to succeed Moses in their mission of establishing Israel as a permanent civilization. Like Moses, Joshua became not just the Hebrews' religious leader but an effective military strategist. His military conquests were many, but it is his famous quotation that everyone mentions when his name comes up. And it is this: *"Choose you this day whom ye will serve, but as for me and my house, we will serve the Lord."*

Joshua's quotation causes pause: *"What or whom am I serving, and is this what I really want to do with my life?"*

Real Entitlement

Entering this world in total innocence, a child desperately needs two faithful souls—mother and father—to love it, to protect it, to provide for it, and to do so in every way. Everlasting joy flocks to parents thusly dedicated, supporting and sustaining them in their divine project. In addition to the child, also needing an American Mind's faithful service, are spouse, sibling, parent, peer, neighbor, business associate, and fellow citizen. The *Reason* of the cosmos blesses this effort.

A closing quote from Albert: *"Our time is distinguished by wonderful achievements in the fields of scientific understanding and the technical application of those insights. Who would not be cheered by this? But let us not forget that human knowledge and skills alone cannot lead humanity to a happy and dignified life. Humanity has every Reason to place the proclaimers of high moral standards and values above the discoverers of objective truth. What humanity owes to personalities like Buddha, Moses, and Jesus ranks for me higher than all the achievements of the enquiring and constructive mind.*

"What these blessed men have given us we must guard and try to keep alive with all our strength if humanity is not to lose its dignity, the security of its existence, and its joy in living."

And what these blessed men have given us that we must guard and try to keep alive with all our strength, has culminated within the American Mind and the moral pillars upon which it stands.

About the Author

*B*uzz was born in Texas and grew up on a cotton farm in Arizona. Besides being a farmer of renown, Buzz's father was a member of the original Rodeo Cowboys Association. Buzz, too, is a card-carrying cowboy, rodeoing since pre-teen years. It's impossible to know how many hours Buzz spent on a horse growing up, not just rodeoing but punching cattle day after day. Because he has always had a farm/ranch to manage, rodeo was reserved for weekends, never full-time. Like golf, rodeo is a sport, and rodeo cowboys are athletes. Not exactly what Hollywood says they are, but close.

Buzz converted to the Church of Jesus Christ of Latter-Day Saints (Mormon) and served two-plus years as a missionary in Argentina. Working in ghettos shapes one's worldview about which behavioral patterns advance life and which do not. Buzz's life experiences have instructed him well, especially in those aspects of life with the most potential for wholesale accomplishment and happiness.

As a curious fourth-grader, Buzz found his curiosity piqued by a series of books about American presidents. He was particularly interested in the personality traits of those who led the United States of America—especially its greatest leaders. As life progressed and study continued, it became clear to Buzz that a particular worldview formed the minds that built and sustain America as the *beacon on the hill*. Buzz remains an avid student of America's personality.

Professionally, Buzz is a farmer raised by a farmer. As a farmer, he served on the Boards of Directors for the United States Potato Board and the United Potato Growers of America. Retiring from farming, he accepted a position with the United Potato Growers of America headquartered in Salt Lake City. He now serves as COO of UPGA. Buzz currently writes monthly articles for two agricultural publications in addition to producing two weekly agricultural podcasts.

At UPGA's inception, Buzz helped develop a cutting-edge supply/demand/price data system that today receives global recognition. At the request of global agricultural leaders, Buzz and wife, Susan, traveled to England, Belgium, the Netherlands, Germany, France, Canada's eastern provinces, and New Zealand, presenting the data system. While in England, Buzz presented a paper at Cambridge University to leading agricultural economists concerning UPGA's unique supply/demand/pricing strategy and the data system that supports it. Of particular interest to the Cambridge audience was how a group of farmers, without governmental help, changed the business culture of potato production. The change resulted from American thinking, something startling to English and European minds.

Buzz's education consists of two years at Arizona State University, finishing with a BS degree in animal science from Brigham Young University. While completing a B.S. degree at Brigham Young University, Buzz met and married Susan Westover of Sacramento, California. Buzz and Susan have six daughters, six sons-in-law, twenty-three grandchildren, and one great-grandchild. Their sons-in-law hold three JDs, one MD, three MBAs, plus one PhD (taught Harvard

MBAs). Their daughters' educations are similar.

Buzz and Susan reside in Mesa, Arizona, play a lot of golf, and Buzz continues his lifelong, inherited love of horses, competing in team roping events across the Southwest. Buzz and Susan have boxes and boxes of books stored around their home.

Additional Reading

Ambrose, Steven E. *D-Day, June 6, 1944: The Climactic Battle of World War II*. New York: Simon & Schuster, 1994.

Bartlett's Famous Quotations. Boston: Little & Brown, 1992.

Bennett, William. *Index of Leading Cultural Indicators*. New York: Broadway Books, 1999.

Brian, Denis. *Einstein-A Life*. New York: John Wiley & Sons, Inc., 1996.

Bronte, Charlotte. *Jane Eyre*. London: Smith, Elder & Company, 1847.

Chopra, Depak. *The Seven Spiritual Laws of Success*. San Rafael, CA: New World Library, 1994.

Churchill, Winston. *A History of the English Speaking Peoples – The New World*. New York: Dodd, Mead, & Company, 1956.

Coulter, Ann. *Godless – The Church of Liberalism*. New York: Random House, 2006.

Declaration of Independence

DesMaisons, Kathleen. *Potatoes Not Prozac*. New York: Fireside, 1998.

Ellis, Joseph J. *His Excellency George Washington*. New York: Alfred A. Knopf, 2004.

Ford, Worthington Chauncey. *The Writings of Washington*. New York: Putnam's Sons, 1889–93.

Goodwin, Doris. *Team of Rivals*, Simon & Schuster Paperbacks, New York, NY, 2006.

Hobhouse, Henry. *Seeds of Change.* Great Britain: Sedgwick & Jackson, Limited, 1985.

Isaacson, Walter. *Benjamin Franklin: An American Life.* New York: Simon & Schuster, 2003.

Meyer, Stephen. C. *Signature in the Cell; DNA and the Evidence for Intelligent Design*, Harper Collins, 2009

King James Bible

LDS Standard Works

LDS.org

Masters, Roy, Bob Just and Dorothy Baker, eds. *Finding God in Physics: Einstein's Missing Relative (Why We and the Universe Exist).* Grants Pass, OR: Foundation of Human Understanding, 1997.

McCullough, David. *John Adams.* New York: Simon & Schuster, 2001.

Reagan, Ronald. *A Shining City.* New York: Simon & Schuster, 1998.

Steiner, Franklin. *The Religious Beliefs of Our Presidents.* Amherst, NY: Prometheus Books, 1995.

Unger, Harlow Giles. *Patrick Henry: Lion of Liberty.* Da Capo Press, Cambridge, MA, 2010

Warren, Rick. *The Purpose Driven Life.* Grand Rapids, MI: Zondervan, 2002.

The Internet as a Limitless Resource

Biographies as a must:
> *Aristotle, Pythagoras, Ptolemy, Copernicus, Galileo, DaVinci, Kepler, Newton, Pasteur, and Einstein.*
>
> *And: Abraham, Moses, Muhammad, Buddha, Confucius, and Jesus.*
>
> *And: Abraham Lincoln, John Adams, Thomas Jefferson, Ronald Reagan, Harry Truman, Andrew Jackson, Teddy Roosevelt, George Washington, Benjamin Franklin, and Franklin D. Roosevelt.*
>
> *And: Every Other American President.*
>
> *And: Daniel Boone, Frederick Douglass, Quanah Parker, Frank Hamer, Chuck Yeager, Micky Mantle, and . . .*

Ingram Content Group UK Ltd.
Milton Keynes UK
UKHW042225300623
424389UK00001B/63